P9-EDP-198

LIFE Pacific College
Alumni Library
1100 West Covina Blvd.
San Dimas, CA 91773

DATE DUE

JUN 1 6 1980		
MAY 1 0 1982		
NOV 2 8 1983		
DEC 3 1984		
OCT 2 1 1985		
NOV 1 1 1985		
GAYLORD 234		PRINTED IN U. S. A.

L.I.F.E. College Library
1100 Glendale Blvd.
Los Angeles, Calif. 90026

OF
WISE MEN
AND FOOLS

OF
WISE MEN
AND FOOLS

Realism in the Bible

16384

David Edman

Introduction by Kenneth L. Wilson

L.I.F.E. College Library
1100 Glendale Blvd.
Los Angeles, Calif. 90026

DOUBLEDAY & COMPANY, INC., GARDEN CITY, NEW YORK 1972

L.I.F.E. College Library
1100 Glendale Blvd.
Los Angeles, Calif. 90026

Library of Congress Catalog Card Number 76-180072
Copyright © 1972 by David Edman
All Rights Reserved
Printed in the United States of America
First Edition

Excerpts from THE NEW ENGLISH BIBLE. © the Delegates of the
Oxford University Press and the Syndics of the Cambridge University
Press 1961, 1970. Reprinted by permission.

Excerpts from "Bees in Amber" copyright American Tract Society,
1908. Reprinted in Protestant Episcopal Hymnal 1940, p. 263.

Excerpts from THE REVISED STANDARD VERSION OF THE
BIBLE, Copyrighted 1946 and 1952.

20.92
540

LIFE Pacific College
Alumni Library
1100 West Covina Blvd.
San Dimas, CA 91773

CONTENTS

Contents vii

The Question of Gentile Converts . . .
Differing Opinions on Mark

XI. Luke the Unknown   202

A Penchant for Obscurity . . . What Luke
Omitted . . . Some Unconscious Self-
Revelations . . . The Writing of Luke and
Acts

FOR EVELYN

INTRODUCTION

This is not a book that needs an introduction, any more than one must be introduced to a hearty meal. All that needs to be said is, "Come and get it!" Those who are hungry will come and those who are not won't, and not even an admirer of the cook can create an appetite. All he can do is express his own appreciation of samplings of the menu and try to get the juices flowing.

I feel responsible for this book to about the same degree that the fellow who said to Columbus, "Why don't you sail out that way?" could be said to have discovered America. For after I had read the first two or three articles of what became a popular *Christian Herald* series, "Bible Stories Retold," I encouraged David Edman to write a book. Not that there is a lack of books about the Bible, which is probably the most overbooked topic in history. This one is different, and let me see if on the way to the table I can explain why I think so.

It all has to do with our state of mind regarding the Bible, a book so special, so timeless, that, unlike any other, it is known as God's Word. Most people are willing to give it preferred status, a passing nod, but that's about as far as it goes; reading it is something else.

Many of those who do read it are so terribly serious

about the Bible that they've taken all the fun out of what can be a delightful experience. For them, Bible reading is looked upon as an act of devotion that somehow gratifies God even if it leaves them confused and unfulfilled. The rationale is that if God feels good enough he will dispense some personal blessing, or, at the national level, nudge the Dow-Jones average up five or ten points and that reading the Bible is one sure-fire way to improve his disposition. Even if we do not enjoy Bible reading or get anything much out of it, the exhorters hint, "prayer and Bible reading" nevertheless constitute an inseparable chore and teach us discipline if nothing else. It is the doing of it, they imply, that is good for the soul, not necessarily the enjoying or understanding of it—a measure we are not likely to apply to any other kind of reading.

Then there are others who assure us that the Bible has "the answers," as if the problems are scattered around in life with the notation, "See answer on page 63," and there it is, printed upside down so it won't be too easy. Does it really matter very much that the Bible is the best seller or how many versions or translations we own or how reverently we display a copy of it or even how much of it we read or how often we read it, if all we're doing is penance or puzzles?

"Well," one hears the cliché, "what you get out of it depends upon what you put into it." However, it's not "what" you put into it that provides the relevance, but "whom" you put into it, and the most important "whom" is yourself. The awe with which both readers and non-readers approach the Bible makes it almost impossible for us to put ourselves into it, which is to say, to identify with Bible characters.

For those who people its pages have seemed to be extraordinary, a race of beings apart from us mortals. They, unlike us, appear to have done mostly the right things at the right times. When they did blunder, it all came out right anyway. They seem to have lived charmed lives. And so those of us looking on received the mistaken impression that God was calling the shots for them and they couldn't lose (except the ones like Judas who were born losers).

How can you and I identify with supermen like that? We can't possibly get ourselves into the picture when they were so strong and we are so weak, when they were so sure of themselves and we are so unsure, when their faith was so unshakable and ours so tormented. David Edman's great contribution is that he gives you a hand-up at getting into the Bible. He makes it possible for us to feel at home with men and women who, in their own ways, had to cope with uncertainty, just as we do. Their lives look ordered and orderly only because we know how their story turned out, though they themselves did not and could not know. Anybody can be strong in retrospect, but the human beings of the Bible did not live in retrospect, any more than we do as far as our own lives are concerned. It is the present tense that provides our anxieties—and that provided theirs. David Edman restores the present tense and the present tensions to the lives of a sampling of saints and sinners.

One can identify with a Solomon who made his share of mistakes, for we make our own share. One can identify even with a Judas who was not evil personified but a tired little bookkeeper-type who did the financial worrying for all the Disciples. I don't know about you, but I can't identify with anyone who was totally good or totally bad—and the characters of the Bible weren't either.

The lack of press agentry in the Bible is one of its remarkable—and self-authenticating—qualities. That any of us ever felt we needed to apologize for its shattering realism and searching objectivity is a disquieting commentary on our understanding of Scriptural loyalty. We have made of Biblical heroes figures more heroic than the Bible itself makes of them, and to the extent that we did it, we whittled away at Biblical relevance.

The essays in this book do not diminish the Bible. Indeed, by letting its characters be more fully human, they let God be more divine, for it becomes clear that he accomplished his purpose not because he found men who were angelic but because he used men who were not. So this is a reverent book, giving credit where credit is due—to the artist, not to the paint. That God could make something out of the material he had to work with then, gives us hope that perhaps he can make something out of the material he has to work with today, namely, you and me.

New York   Kenneth L. Wilson

I THE BIBLE:
FOR ADULTS MOSTLY

We think so because other people think so,
Or because—or because—after all we do think so,
Or because we were told so, and think we must think so,
Or because we once thought so, and think we still think so,
Or because having thought so, we think we *will* think so.

—Henry Sidgwick

We might begin with a bit of nostalgia.

Picture, if you would, the Sunday school class you attended when you were in, say, the fourth grade. Imagine that there before you once more is the old table which came up to your chin. Around it are a circle of those devilishly painful wooden chairs, yellow in color, folding in nature, with a patent disdain for human comfort in every angle and plane. Nearby stands the upright piano which long ago was painted a light blue by some palsied volunteer.

Over on one wall you can still see the attendance chart with its constellation of gummed stars. Thumbtacked to the wall opposite are a number of rather brownish reproductions of Biblical paintings. Underneath stands a donated, which is to say discarded, bookshelf on top of which rests the wooden box filled with a mixture of crayon ends and those miniature scissors especially designed to lacerate the first joint of your thumb. Next to it is the ever present pile of construction paper. Over all there abides the pervasive odor of mildew and white paste.

Presiding over the class is dear old Miss Everlasting, or so we shall for convenience name her. She is a kindly Victorian light. No one knows her age, nor quite how long she has been teaching Sunday school. You have been told that she taught your father some years back, and, so far as can be determined, your grandfather as well. You also are aware that she taught them the same material she is presently teaching you, and in exactly the same manner. Finally you presume, without thinking much about it, that in some future year she will be teaching your children yet to come.

Dear old Miss Everlasting! From her lips you learned the wonderful stories of the Bible. They were well told. Miss Everlasting was an excellent narrator. From the way she told those stories you almost felt that she was an eyewitness to the events she was describing, a conjecture not far from wrong. Through her storytelling abilities the characters of the Bible came to be a part of your imaginary world. Along with the others in the cast of your fantasies there were Noah with his floating zoo, David with his trusty slingshot, Mary demure and obedient, Daniel relaxed among the lions.

Whatever was lacking in Miss Everlasting's description of the people and places of the Bible was made up for by the holy pictures which supplemented the spoken word. Who could possibly forget the fuzzy lithographs which interleaved the pages of those black, hard-backed class Bibles? All one had to do was to open to the glossy pages, turn the Bible sideways, and there was the boy Samuel in that mysterious temple, or Joseph being carted off to Egypt, or the baby Moses being discovered in the bulrushes by Pha-

raoh's raven-haired daughter, or Nebuchadnezzar and his sky-
scraper of a fiery furnace, or Christ among the firkins at
the marriage in Cana.

No one I knew of in my day ever showed the slightest
skepticism at the artist's depiction of life in the Holy Land.
We assumed that the pictures were authentic illustrations of
what it was like to be alive in those days. Every one of
us supposed that the people who lived in Biblical times
wore sandals and white flowing undergarments and striped
bathrobes. We also took it for granted that the people
of Israel had rather Anglo-Saxon features, that they always
managed to look freshly laundered, that they were tanned
and fit and possessed of perfect sets of teeth and well-
trimmed hair and beards.

It did not even seem strange that these people lived
in a kind of Arcadian splendor. Who could know that the
plant life of those pictures was rarely that of the Middle
East? The trees we gazed upon were not the scrubby affairs
of the Levant, but rather huge deciduous affairs, the sort of
massive shade trees that one associates with an English
landscape by Turner. The paths were tidy curving affairs
which led through sylvan glades and over immaculate greens.
The hills in the distance were gently rounded, and the sheep
which grazed upon them unbelievably white. Occasionally
here and there could be seen the homes of people, which
always had a way of looking rather like typical American
mausoleums.

We looked at these pictures and listened to Miss Everlasting's stories of the Bible, and we became convinced of
two things. First, we were certain that these people actually
did live at one time in the land of Israel under the
circumstances described. They were presented to us as
genuinely historical people, and none of us had the critical
faculties, much less the audacity, to assume otherwise.

But of something else we were also convinced. Namely,
that these people did not resemble anyone *we* knew. If
anything, they were more like the characters of the fairy
and adventure stories which were also a part of our milieu.
The story of David and Goliath, for example, was not
entirely dissimilar to that of Jack and the Beanstalk. Daniel
seemed rather like a character out of the Arabian Nights.
Noah was more or less of an antediluvian Doctor Doolittle,
and the Disciples were vaguely comparable to the Knights
of the Round Table.

The truth of it is, then, that the reality of those Biblical
characters did not entirely come through. We believed in
them all right, but it was an immature belief, a conditional
belief, the condition being a childlike credulity that such
people once existed, even if they exist no longer.

Still, it didn't much matter how real they might have
seemed, for while they may have been presented to us as
historical characters, they were not depicted with much
in the way of realism. Rather they were served up to us
more on the order of moral caricatures than anything else.
Each character tended to have a virtue or vice attached,
as obvious as a tag on a new suit. One Biblical character
was supposed to teach us the value of perseverance, another
of loyalty, another of faith, another of honesty, and so
forth. In short, these people were embalmed in moralisms.
They were the stock characters of episodes whose conclusions
went: "Now the *moral* of the story is . . ." Consequently,
they either tended to be amazingly virtuous, or utterly
depraved and villainous. They were described as either
the loyal allies of God, or the very agents of the devil.

It is not difficult to understand why this was so. Sunday
school instruction was keyed on the ethical. We were being
taught to be virtuous and no problem to our parents. We
ended the morning by pledging in song to be "always kind

and good." Hence it was a matter of practicality to present the Bible as a moral primer, and its characters as types of good and evil.

That Miss Everlasting's method of using the Bible had certain short-term advantages might be arguable. Without casting discredit on either her devotedness or her intentions, we must point out that in principle it was certainly a misuse of the Scriptures. Nevertheless, it provided many happy hours as well as some elementary moral guidance.

The long-range effects of this utilization of the Bible, however, tend to be much more open to question, as we shall now see.

THE HAZARDS OF SUNDAY SCHOOL

However fondly we look back on that old Sunday school class (or catechism class, or Sabbath school), we must not forget that, like all childhood experiences, Sunday school had certain bad potentials as well as good. Some pupils, for example, found Sunday school boring, and concluded at a very early age that religion in general was boring and that the church was the place to go when one wanted to be bored. Others found the materials taught in Sunday school too sentimental and idealistic to be of any practical use in a world of bullies and incessant competition and parents who were by turn unaccountably solicitous and irritable.

But of all dangers inherent in that old Sunday school class, none was quite so hazardous, in retrospect, as the possibility that this brief episode of religious education at the primary level would be the end of it, that Sunday school would come to provide a person's one and only acquaintance with the Bible.

Unfortunately, too often this proved to be the case. There seems to be no shortage of people in the world whose experience with the Bible was abruptly terminated at the age of eleven or twelve, and whose religious attitudes thereafter became correspondingly petrified. Because of this, many a person, mature in every other way, has gone through life with an understanding of the Bible and Biblical religion which can only be described as puerile.

Such arrested religious development has often proved to be a person's religious undoing, for it has deprived him of a mature and adequate faith during times of personal crisis. Under conditions when faith must, as it were, *produce,* many people have found themselves saddled with the alternative of either trying to content themselves with a childish religion, or discarding it altogether.

What makes such a dilemma as this pitiable is that it is so unnecessary. There is no good reason why a person's intellect needs be shackled by an infantile view of religion. Granted one is supposed to possess a childlike faith. But it should be recognized that this is not quite the same as a child*ish* faith. There is a world of difference between a serene, uncomplicated set of religious convictions and one which is immature.

In many respects, the problem being described here emanates from an inadequate comprehension of the Bible. Since the Bible provides the basis for most religion practiced in western culture, popular attitudes concerning it are determinative.

It seems only plausible, therefore, that it is with the Bible that a part of the solution is to be found. The prescription also seems obvious enough. Inadequate ideas about the Bible must give way to informed ones. Childish views of Biblical religion must be replaced by those of maturity and judgment.

Perhaps there is no better way of disabusing ourselves of certain of the more pernicious attitudes regarding the Bible than reminding ourselves of three evident facts about the Bible and the use thereof.

1. THE BIBLE WAS NOT INTENDED FOR CHILDREN.

This particular statement scarcely needs to be buttressed. That the writers, editors, compilers, redactors, canonizers and translators of the Bible engaged in their work primarily so that children could be provided with religious instruction is patently absurd.

Despite this, what is the principle use to which the Bible is put? That of a moral textbook for children. Who would care to argue otherwise? One need not cite statistics, but merely ask the reader to examine his own experience. For the great majority of people, their only prolonged exposure to the Bible was that provided by Miss Everlasting. This occupied a good part of that period of childhood known as latency. Then, with the onset of puberty, the enthusiasm for the Bible which she generated tended to wane as youthful minds were given to other matters, notably the existence of the other sex. After that the Bible became the great closed book—unless, of course, one was later prevailed upon to teach a Sunday school class himself.

It is through this pattern of childhood usage and adult neglect that there has grown up the widespread and ghastly assumption that the Bible is primarily a tool of elementary religious instruction. Active church members, even, tend to regard the sixty-six books of the Old and New Testaments as little more than a compendium of moral truisms which ought to be crammed into young minds before encountering the manifold temptations of adulthood.

There is a hidden side to this assumption too. It is the
suspicion that the Bible has little to offer adults. The Bible
is conceived as being one of those books which occupies
one's childhood, then outgrown. Such a belief is seldom ar-
ticulated, but it is almost universally acted upon; for, as is
generally known, while family Bibles are often displayed,
they are rarely read.

The truth about the Bible is quite opposite, prevailing
opinions notwithstanding. The Bible was certainly not written
for children. Indeed, it is not even very suitable for children,
a fact which is neither radical nor even surprising. It is
more on the order of one of those cool facts which almost
any thinking adult will agree to after a few moments of
reflection. Any Biblical scholar will tell you that the amount
of material in the Bible which can—in a direct and exeget-
ically honest fashion—be imparted to children is negligible.
If one's mind skips over the major parts of the Bible,
the fact grows even more incontrovertible. The Pentateuch
is not particularly suited to the instruction of children for
self-evident reasons. The historical parts of the Old Testament, the so-called "Former Prophets" are generally too
primitive and bloodthirsty. Only a very few of the Psalms
and other "Writings" can be appreciated by children. The
prophets are way out of reach. As for the New Testament,
one can rule out the Apostle Paul from the outset, as he
hardly demonstrates much concern in making himself clear
to pre-pubescent minds. And it is only in the most restricted
sense that the Gospels can be used for elementary religious
education. For the person who says, "Ah, but what about
the parables?" I would point to Joachim Jeremias' study,
The Parables of Jesus, for an appreciation of their essential
complexity.

Nor should we shrink from the implication of these facts,
but go further and admit that it is only with great care

and discernment that the Bible should be used at all in the instruction of children. At the level of stories-with-morals-attached it can be perhaps innocuous. But beyond this it can quickly become downright harmful. For example, to teach the great sagas of creation to children as though they were factual historical occurrences almost amounts to inviting that same child, come of age, to dismiss the entire Bible as basically untrue.

The truth of it is that the Bible is for adults. It is to the adult mind that the Bible addresses itself with its message of man's need and God's self-manifestation. It takes an adult mind to grasp the profound typology within the Old Testament sagas of man's emergence to self-consciousness. It is only an adult mind which can savor the momentous human problems which occur in the pages of the Bible. A child, for example, could never grasp the implications of Job's razor-thin escape from atheistic despair, or the strangely out-of-place epicureanism of the book of Ecclesiastes, or the Apostle Paul's monumental effort to disabuse mankind of its perennial belief that religion is primarily the adherence to a set of religious rules.

Again, as we shall shortly examine in greater detail, it is decidedly on an adult level that the Bible sets forth the careers of its characters. Only Shakespeare comes near the Bible in his ability to get close to the heart of man. When the famous British theologian P. T. Forsyth advised preachers to keep both the Bible and Shakespeare close at hand, he was simply commending the two greatest resources on the subject of human nature.

We can only conclude, then, that the way in which the Bible is generally used today is about one hundred and eighty degrees off course. What would make far more sense in our churches would be much less Bible in the religious instruction of children, and far more among adults.

Giving the Bible an "R" rating might not be everyone's philosophy of religious education. Yet the thoughtful reader will not mistake the point being made.

2. THE BIBLE IS ORIENTED TOWARD REALISM.

The point here is an expansion of the foregoing, with more of an emphasis on its positive aspects. It recognizes that while children are oriented toward fantasy and make-believe, the Bible is not. On the contrary, the Bible is an incredibly realistic book.

Pier Paolo Pasolini's *The Gospel according to St. Matthew* helps to make the point. When this film was first shown some years ago, it was extravagantly praised by the more intellectual religious journals. This was not exactly due to the film's intrinsic merits, for while Pasolini depicted the Palestine of Jesus' day with rare art, he never got much beyond a woodenly literalistic interpretation of the text.

Rather, what caused such a general rejoicing was the fact that this low-cost Italian effort to put a segment of the Bible onto celluloid proved such a refreshing change from the standard Hollywood Biblical epics. Gone were the cast of thousands, the Ionian backdrops, the chariot races, the papier-mâché upheavals, the cosmetic miracles, the grandiose characters with their hair and beards in permanent waves. The characters of Pasolini's film—dirty, unshaven, destitute, with ignorance and ache written into the lines of their faces —seemed entirely believable. The arid hot land, too, seemed like the land which Jesus must have trod.

Nor did the chief figure in this motion picture resemble the docetic Christ of Hollywood scenarios, who invariably managed to come across as something on the order of a first-century Mr. Clean. Pasolini's Christ, a mixture of the ordinary and extraordinary, was convincing as a human being in whom existed an awesome and bewildering power. His actions and reactions were the sorts of things one would expect of an incarnate deity.

The disciples too, confused and ill-kempt, had an air of authenticity about them. As a result, the viewers felt that this particular film director had managed to reach out and touch the Gospel at several points. For this he received some much-deserved credit.

When contrasted to Pasolini's contribution, the Hollywood productions were seen for what they in fact are: childish. What many of us dimly suspected surfaced to consciousness: to wit, that there was something rather Sunday-schoolish about them. Indeed, these mawkish productions bore an undeniably close relationship to the lessons of Miss Everlasting. As in her tellings of the Bible stories, the figures in these technicolor extravaganzas tended to be moral caricatures—either very virtuous or very villainous. The backgrounds in which they operated were idealized and sterile. The dialogues were inane, the plots simplistic, the theology incredible. By any reasonable analysis, Cecil B. De Mille and his imitators seemed more like Sunday school storytellers gone berserk than film artists. One even wonders if it is too cynical to suggest that what these producers managed to do was to cash in on the public's generally stunted knowledge of the Bible, for a film with Victor Mature as Samson gadding about ornate Philistine palaces or a Charlton Heston as Moses conducting the movements of the Red Sea like a Viennese maestro in fact depends for its financial success on great numbers of people with very infantile views of the Scriptures.

The gravest injury accorded the Bible by these commercialized ventures was that done to its essential realism. What the scenario writers either did not, or could not, know is that the Bible is unswervingly oriented toward a realistic understanding of the world. There is little romantic about the Bible. Its stories, for the most part, are not idyllic, its message not a collection of insipid moral clichés, its characters not a cast of melodramatic stereotypes.

Nowhere is this realism more evident than in the over-all depiction of the people of the Bible. Very rarely does one find in the Bible a caricature—which is to say, a one-dimensional character who serves to make a point. The Bible assumes the complexity of man. Rarely does it fail to respect the fact that the human individual is an extremely contra-dictory being. It senses that deep within him jostle all sorts of curious and bizarre ambivalences. It acknowledges that man is at once proud and craven, rebellious and submissive, lordly and puny, tragic and comic, cowardly and courageous, loving and spiteful.

It must be emphasized that there is nothing accidental about the realism with which the Bible sets forth its char-acters. This approach stems from a theological conviction more than anything else. It is based upon Israel's age-old belief that between God and man there exists a radical separation. In the Bible, God is God, and man is man, and the two are not to be confused either in role or attributes. On the one hand there is the perfect Creator— a majestically simple and omniscient being. Though created in the spiritual image of God, man represents a distinct contrast. He is created. He is fallen. He is limited. He is confused. He wallows in contradictions. God may be uncom-plicated, but man is not. Thus, for a man to be depicted as having the characteristics of God—as, for instance, by describing a man as possessing some sort of moral perfec-tion—is in the Biblical mind to be guilty of that most heinous of religious errors, idolatry.

Consequently one finds in the Bible a theological *insistence* to treat all humans, no exceptions, with brutal honesty. The Biblical writers made little effort to gloss over the negative features of their heroes. They were described pointedly and unapologetically, virtues and vices alike. This was because these writers were prevented by their religion from deifying their religious and political leaders. They had no recourse but the truth, even when it was painful. And so they chronicled the doings of their people with literally religious accuracy; and if this meant that their kings had to be depicted as renegades, their prophets as charlatans, their heroes as fools, then they were so depicted.

One cannot help compare this candid approach with that of the Hollywood epic. The wide-screen versions of Israel's heroes have a way of being almost grotesquely singular in their delineation of character, an interpretation quite at odds with that of the Bible itself. For there nearly every person has a way of turning out a veritable potpourri of mingled virtues and vices. To understand this is not to be surprised when the saga of the Flood ends with a drunken Noah, or to find an *im*patient Job cursing and blaspheming, or to learn that Samuel was a political intriguer, David a roué and Solomon a fool.

It is just such incredible candor which gives the Bible its never-ending fascination. It can be argued that one of the reasons the Bible retains its vitality, while the other religious literatures being composed around the same time have all but been forgotten, is that these others were essentially a heroic literature whose characters were dull stereotypes. Anyone who has an acquaintance with the religious writings which emerged from the civilizations of Mesopotamia, Egypt, Greece and Rome know that these were largely legendary accounts of the deeds of gods and demigods and heroes. These characters bore only the most incidental relationship to common life. As a consequence they are stale, uninteresting literary figures, fit only for the dustier archives of comparative religion.

The Bible, on the other hand, survives as an intensely human document. And what, after all, can be more enticing

than the study of humanity in all of its glory and wretched-
ness?

George H. Morrison, a Scottish preacher of a few generations back, was moved to express gratitude for the Bible's
unadorned presentation of its characters in this way:

> I can never be thankful enough to the Almighty for the
> exceeding frankness of the Bible. If God had hidden the failings
> of His children, or sketched them with a halo round their heads
> as in the dull lives of the mediaeval saints, we should long
> since have shut this Bible, and let the dust gather on its
> boards.

3. THE BIBLE REQUIRES STUDY.

There is only one way by which childish attitudes about
the Bible can give way to a mature understanding. That is
through the discipline of study. Unfortunately there are no
shortcuts here. Without a broad understanding of the Bible's
background, one is doomed to either a childish understanding of it, or total ignorance.

Nevertheless, before being turned away by the word
"study," the reader should remind himself that in general
people are not only willing, but actually quite eager to study
the things which interest them. A man interested in professional football has no difficulty in concentrating his attention on tables of football statistics. Likewise, a woman who
has developed a concern for the political process and becomes active in such an organization as the League of
Women Voters will gladly involve herself in the research
necessary to her interest. Even a student who flunks out of
high school because of a passion for souped-up jalopies
has merely neglected one form of study for another.

The point so obviously being made here is that any person

who is sincerely interested in the Bible, or has become convinced that it is a source of divine guidance, should not be troubled by the requirement of study.

The reason for the necessity of Biblical study can be briefly given. Far from being a collection of pleasant stories and mottoes suitable for framing, the Bible is a vast and disparate collection of sacred writings which was compiled over a period of some thirteen hundred years. Stop for a moment and consider the implications of such a span of time as this! Then reflect that behind the various written documents exist any number of oral traditions which are still older and more diffuse. Without some idea of these backgrounds and the manner in which the Bible came to be compiled, a person cannot hope to comprehend the material he is reading except in a most superficial manner.

Among other requirements, any knowledgeable reading of the Bible must surely recognize that the Bible was written within the context of a cultural and world outlook far different from our own. It was a time when men were more tightly hemmed in by their ignorance (though it must be allowed that their understanding of human nature has not been much improved on during the intervening centuries). Men of Biblical times were limited in their knowledge of both the macrocosm, the universe beyond their ken, and the microcosm, the subvisual world. They had no idea of the cause of natural phenomena like earthquakes, volcanoes, eclipses and so on. They were unable to fathom the bacterial and viral agents which cause infection and disease. Naturally they tried to account for these various phenomena, and did so in a quite different manner than that employed by the scientific method of recent centuries. It is because of such disparate explanations of the various forces which impinge themselves on human existence that an eminent scholar of our times, Rudolf Bultmann, has called for a "demythologization" of the Bible.

Beyond a general knowledge of the condition of the Biblical world and mind lie the old exegetical demands. Exegesis—a most important term for those who would study the Bible—refers to the attempt to clarify with utmost precision the exact and original meaning of a particular Biblical passage. In a sense the exegetical process involves the old newspaper writers' interrogatory: who, when, what and why. In the case of a verse or chapter from the Bible, *who* wrote it, and to whom? *When* was this passage written, and what were the world or local conditions at the time? *What* form of writing (letter, sermon, poetry, saga, etc.) did the author employ? And *why* did he write? What purpose did he have in mind?

Any person who has a grasp of the information demanded by such questions should have little difficulty in comprehending the passage of Scripture at hand.

Doubtless there are some who would protest this approach. Two broad forms of objection come to mind. First would be that of those who have a deeply religious attachment to the Bible's authority over the hearts and minds of men. The objections here would center on the making of the Bible one object of study among others. Such treatment of the Bible, they would say, is too rational, too cold-blooded, indeed too demeaning and irreverent. They would suspect that an objective study of the Bible would interfere with one's belief in its inspiration. Or they might be inclined to refer to some sainted grandmother who, they say, read the Bible every day and knew more about it than any seminary professor.

It is rather difficult to engage such objections as these, largely because they rest upon a set of prior assumptions about the Bible which are held with great feeling. These assumptions are focused about a general belief that the Bible is God's most direct means of communicating with individual men. People who hold them feel that the Bible functions much on the order of an oracle and therefore ought to be consulted, not studied. Such an attitude lay behind a remark once made to me: "I don't bother with commentaries. I go directly to the 'Word.'"

Such views are often held by persons of a very devout and sincere nature. Nevertheless before ruling out the importance of Biblical scholarship, they should examine their own presuppositions, asking such questions as: How could the study of Biblical backgrounds do anything *but* help in its understanding? Is not understanding itself a kind of inspiration? Does not the concept of simultaneously meaningful and unexamined Scriptures imply a very capricious doctrine of God?

Also, one should be careful not to rule out in advance the possibility of reading the Bible in a way which is both knowledgeable *and* reverent. Such a combination, for example, was much in evidence in the life of the noted British scholar Bishop Westcott of Durham. In a letter of 1872, Henry Scott Holland, later a canon of St. Paul's, described a visit to this great Biblical critic:

> He is the sort of man before whose high-toned purity and prayerfulness and intense religiousness I cower with shame. He prays with us when we come to him; so slowly, gently, whisperingly. He speaks of St. John's Gospel with a sort of hushed awe: it is like Fra Angelico, he cannot venture to criticise a verse without a prayer.

The other type of objection might come from those who have become alienated from religion altogether. Theirs would focus on the burdensome nature of the study of the Bible, or perhaps its assumed irrelevency. There are many who, without any investigation of the matter whatsoever, have concluded that the study of the Bible is a dull and futile exercise, fit only for fanatics and eggheads.

I would hope that in some small measure this book would

help disabuse people of this idea. Actually the Bible can be a great joy to study for believers and unbelievers alike, for it is a magnificent document, unique in world history, and of incalculable influence on it. The way to the study of the Bible has been made easy by generations of devoted scholars. Their labors have made it possible for any literate person to quickly achieve the mental wherewithal by which this remarkable book can be both understood and appreciated.

There are any number of excellent books available for the study of the Bible. Indeed there are so many that it would be difficult to put together a representative bibliography. Let it suffice here to note that much basic information about the Bible can be secured from the twelve volumes of *The Interpreter's Bible* and the four volumes of *The Interpreter's Dictionary of the Bible*. These are handsome sets of reference books for any family library, and quite reasonably priced. Much of the more pertinent data contained in these resources has been gathered together and updated in the recently published *The Interpreter's One-Volume Commentary on the Bible*.

OF WISE MEN AND FOOLS

In the pages to follow, the reader will find ten essays on various personalities of the Bible—seven from the Old Testament and three from the New. These have been arranged in a more or less chronological fashion, though there is no particular significance to the sequence I have employed other than the general practicality of moving in this direction.

If there is any one theme which binds these essays together, it could be said to be the attempt to get behind the conventional and frequently childish presentations of these various persons, and to describe them in a manner conducive to the theological outlook of the Bible. Further, if there is any one hope which the author attaches to this book, it is that its readers will be helped to a new attitude about, and appreciation for, the Bible, together with a desire for a more intimate acquaintance with it.

In writing about these Biblical characters, I have attempted to be guided by the three reminders just discussed. To begin with, each essay has been the result of a judicious amount of study. These personalities, nevertheless, have not been set forth in an especially studious manner. In depicting them, I have depended in no small measure on whatever powers of imagination happen to be at my disposal. Still, I have made a conscious effort to bridle my imagination with the facts, and always to signal the reader when I have left the area of the factual for that of the conjectural or speculative.

In accordance with another of the criteria, I have made a deliberate effort to present these personalities in an adult manner—and not what I would conceive to be my own, either. The adult manner referred to is that peculiar to the Bible itself. Many readers will have a vague remembrance of some of these characters from their Sunday school days. They will not for a moment, however, fail to recognize the difference in approach. What is important to realize is that the method here is much closer to what I believe to be the mature character of the Bible itself, and far different from that which prevailed in the old church basement.

Finally, considerable attention has been given to the prevailing realism of the Bible. Nowhere is that realism more evident than in the Biblical treatment of human character. As paradoxical as it may sound, the most striking thing about Biblical personalities is that they seem so ordinary. The circumstances in which they found themselves may have been unusual, to be sure. But they themselves are generally set forth in such a manner that no one could mistake them as being anything but flesh and blood instances of common

humanity. And is it not this combination—ordinary persons
under extraordinary circumstances—which gives the Bible,
and indeed all great literature, its vitality?

The trouble with those larger than life figures of childhood
moral preachments is that after a time they grew boring.
The saccharine hero and dastardly villain eventually lost
our interest. What may have been useful in childhood religious
instruction became flat and uninteresting as we grew older.
Life was not presented to us in these terms, so we shrugged
them aside.

What many of us failed to realize later on is that we didn't
get the story right. The people of the Bible *weren't* like
that! Not at all! Rather they breathed life. It is the genius
of the Bible that although the persons who crowd its pages
lived thousands of years ago, they were presented with such
realism that it is not at all difficult to imagine them as being
alive today. Their cosmic outlook may have differed from
ours. But their basic patterns of behavior, their desires, their
fears, their appetites and inclinations—all of the things which
truly count in any assessment of human character—these
seem as up-to-date as this morning's newspaper.

One final estimate. It is based on the observation that
truth depends on consistency more than anything else. One
assumes the truth of what an individual says about one
matter by the integrity with which he handles others.

This criterion seems applicable to the Bible too. Its monumental assertions—about God, about the Kingdom, about the
incarnate Revelation—all of these can be accepted only at
the level of personal faith. These assertions are staggering—
staggering in their implications, staggering in their demands.
Yet they are given plausibility by a homelier form of truth;
to wit, the great integrity with which the characters who
inhabit its pages are presented.

II JACOB:
GOD'S ROGUE

In the year of grace 1654, November 23rd, Feast of Clement, Pope and Martyr . . . from about half past ten until half after midnight—FIRE—God of Abraham, God of Isaac, God of Jacob, and not of the philosophers and men of science. . . .

> —from a parchment found sewn inside the coat of Blaise Pascal

Any way you read them, the so-called Jacob-Israel narratives which comprise a good part of the book of Genesis reveal an outrageous rogue. Such, apparently, was Jacob, the third of the patriarchs, the man whose twelve sons would come to be regarded as the founders of the twelve tribes of Israel.

The traditions about Jacob come from many sources. The northern kingdom, Israel, had its own peculiar set of Jacob stories, and so did Judah in the south. The various strands were combined into the narrative as we find it in the first book of the Bible some five hundred years before the birth of Christ.

To the perceptive reader it may seem a little curious that this venerable Hebrew ancestor was not treated with more respect. One would expect the Biblical editors to have engaged in a little whitewashing here and there. Yet there seems to be very little of it. And it is a part of the wonder of

Scriptures that there isn't more! Those Biblical collators must
have winced occasionally as they tied the various anecdotes
about Jacob together. They were proud of their forebears,
and concerned to show them in their best light. But for all
of the right theological reasons they refused to tamper with
the essence of the narratives. What remained after they had
finished, then, was a splendid literary treatment of the rakish
exploits of this, the black sheep of the patriarchs.

How his descendants must have relished the stories about
Jacob! How they must have laughed at this forefather who
personified so many of the Semitic traits and tendencies!
Like Jacob, the Israelites were usurpers—he of his brother
Esau's estate, they of the land of Canaan. Like him they
were shrewd, wily bargainers—as they were bound to be,
living in the unstable region between the dynasties of Egypt
and Mesopotamia. Like Jacob they often acted despicably.
Yet God chose Jacob for his purposes, and God chose them.

People often do a terrible injustice to this part of the
book of Genesis by treating it in a pious or wooden manner.
Without being aware of it, they greatly misuse the Jacob-
Israel stories by failing to see in them the rollicking, scandal-
ous humor that peeps out from nearly every incident in the
life of this all-too-human character.

According to the Bible, Jacob possessed a mixture of many
human virtues, and even more human follies. He was clever,
egotistical, opportunistic and ruthless. He was not above
preying on the distress of others, nor fabricating the most
heinous lies when it suited him. And yet despite his manifest
deficiencies he had at least two profound religious experiences
and, when he felt like it, he could be as pious as a parson.
He knew love and tragedy, gain and loss. And, at the end
of a very long life, he could look back and say that he had
lived in every sense of the term.

A combined Machiavelli and Falstaff, with a pinch of

Don Juan and Till Eulenspiegel thrown in, Jacob was a rogue—God's rogue. And it remains one of the delightful ironies of Christianity that ours is not only the God of Abraham and Isaac; he is the God of Jacob as well.

Without further preliminaries, let us proceed at once to the story of Jacob. In recounting it, we shall make every effort to liberate it from its traditional Sunday school ethos, and to get back to its more original intent: to unfold ancient truths in an entertaining and good humored manner. Perhaps it is best to do so by dividing the story into six parts.

JACOB SWINDLES ESAU

The story of Jacob begins with his bitter sibling rivalry with his elder twin Esau. With characteristic exaggeration, the Hebrew storytellers have the two battling within the very womb of their mother, the aged Rebekah. Esau emerges into the world first, thus securing the rights of eldest heir. But grasping Jacob follows, clutching his brother's heel.

The two are not identical twins, either physically or mentally. Esau bears the characteristics of the Edomite nomads and hunters to the north and east of Canaan. He is ruddy of complexion, hairy and hefty.

Jacob, on the other hand, seems more the pastoral type. One gets the impression that he is more intelligent, more civilized than his brother, though less muscular.

As eldest scion, even though only by a few moments, Esau becomes automatically eligible to all of the prerogatives of the firstborn in a Hebrew household; that is, to be the principal inheritor of the estate, and the one through whom the family name and line is passed. Clearly he is his father's favorite, while Jacob, the baby, remains the darling of his mother.

The narrators make it clear that from the outset Jacob is dissatisfied with his role as number two. His clear intention by fair means or foul is to take his brother's place.

The first opportunity arises on a day when the two have apparently reached young manhood. Returning from an unsuccessful hunt, Esau finds his brother boiling a red, savory stew. Convinced that he is about to die of starvation (a feeling not uncommon among adolescents), Esau asks Jacob for a helping.

Jacob responds in a most unfraternal way. Rather than generously sharing his provisions with Esau, Jacob demands payment. In fact, he demands Esau's privileges as firstborn, his birthright.

In desperation, the famished Esau agrees. Possibly he does not take the demand seriously. Perhaps he deems it another of his brother's perverse whims. Maybe Jacob is playing one more of his practical jokes.

Whatever his estimate of the situation, when the time comes for the birthright to be passed along, Esau indicates no memory of any such agreement. It is a point worth remembering that when Esau is told to prepare for the rite of blessing he does so without any thought of Jacob.

JACOB DECEIVES ISAAC

When it comes time to assume the patriarchal rights, things do not work out for poor Esau in the way he anticipated. This part of the story has all the flavor of a medieval fabliau.

One day Isaac has a premonition that he is about to die. (Actually Isaac did not die for many years to come, but perhaps he is a hypochondriac.) He summons Esau to his presence and orders him to go out on a hunt. When he has achieved success, Isaac tells his eldest son, he is to take his catch and prepare a banquet. The highlight of that banquet, Isaac promises, will be the conferring of the coveted birthright.

Rebekah, who by this time seems to have changed from a lovely young maiden into a scheming old shrew, happens to overhear the conversation. She immediately finds Jacob and persuades him to deceive the nearly blind old man by pretending that he is Esau.

Jacob offers a few token protests, then sets to work on the masquerade with all the élan he can muster—which is not the first time, incidentally, nor the last, that a mother and son have ganged up on a father.

Dressed in the gamey clothes of Esau, fur on neck and forearms to simulate his hirsute twin, Jacob brazenly conveys an ersatz hunter's stew into the presence of his father and there passes himself off as Esau and demands the birthright.

It indicates the amount of intrigue which must have been generated by fraternal discord in this particular household that Isaac instantly becomes suspicious. How, he asks, has the food been obtained so quickly?

Jacob responds with an outright lie—a lie made all the more shocking because he invests it with the providence of God. "Because," he says, "the Lord your God granted me success."

Even this blasphemous assertion fails to convince Isaac. Something, he senses, is wrong. This person here before him demanding his rights seems to be an impostor. In fact it sounds very much like that impossible Jacob.

So Isaac feels the person. Yes. The arms and neck seem hairy enough. Then he smells him. *Smells* like Esau all right, who is always running around the hills and rarely takes a bath.

Yet he asks once more, "Are you really my son Esau?"

"Yes," prevaricates Jacob, "I am."

Once the irrevocable blessing of his father has been secured, Jacob prudently decides to vacate the premises rather than

face the ire of his elder twin. With a hasty good-bye to the
mother he will never see again, Jacob flees to the distant
home of his uncle Laban.

On the way to Haran, the region in which Laban lives,
Jacob undergoes a profound religious experience. Apparently
alone in the wilds east of Jordan, Jacob goes to sleep. His
sleep is understandably troubled. He dreams. And in his
dream he catches a vision of an immense ladder ascending
from earth to heaven. Moving up and down the ladder are
the angels of the Lord God.

It would be impossible to resurrect the significance that
such imagery held for its first hearers. Still one finds in the
vision of Jacob an element which is common to many mystical
insights. What is referred to is the conviction that heaven
may be, in fact, more *real* than earth. Many mystics have
discovered as Jacob did that it is not the abode of man
which is substantial, but rather the abode of God, and earth
is merely its "gate." Here the customary assessment of the
reality of heaven as opposed to earth is reversed. What is
illusory is not heaven, but rather the earth. C. S. Lewis
makes the point imaginatively in his book *The Great Divorce*.
In it he describes earth and hell as shadowy, unreal places.
Yet the reality of heaven is such that the very grass of heaven
is painfully hard to unaccustomed feet.

Jacob is awed by the disclosure. He sets apart the locale of
his mystical experience as a shrine, then journeys on until
he reaches the land of his uncle Laban—quite possibly modern Syria.

Immediately upon arrival he encounters his lovely cousin
Rachel. Jacob promptly falls in love with her, an emotional
attachment which will last all his life.

Jacob is greeted warmly by his relatives. But when it

becomes apparent to Laban that Jacob intends to be something of a perpetual house guest, he prudently offers him a job.

Jacob accepts, then is asked by Laban to name his wages. "Rachel for my wife," replies the infatuated Jacob.

This is acceptable to Laban, though he proposes extremely stiff terms. Jacob, he declares, must put in seven years of hard labor before he can be wed to Rachel. But this is all right with Jacob, for whom no amount of work is to be compared with the beautiful Rachel.

Of course Jacob is being terribly overcharged. Despite the theoretically priceless value of any human being, by any standard of that era, seven years of indentured labor for permission to marry is nothing less than economic gouging at its worst.

The truth of it is that Laban is only getting warmed up. It seems that Rachel has an elder sister named Leah. We are told that she is "weak-eyed." Whether this meant that she was nearsighted and consequently has a tendency to squint, or cross-eyed, or even walleyed, we cannot know. Whatever the precise nature of her disorder, we can be sure that Leah is not about to win any beauty contests.

Nevertheless, it is Leah who provides Jacob with one of the two great surprises of his life. For after seven years of labor and anticipation, the putative wedding to Rachel takes place. Doubtless—for the custom still prevails in parts of the Middle East—the bride is heavily veiled for the ceremony.

Jacob pays little attention. He races through the ritual, then eagerly retires for the commencement of the honeymoon.

Then, *horrors!* Back in the love nest Jacob discovers that it is not the delectable Rachel underneath all those veils. It is *Leah!*

Poor Jacob. He always regarded himself a fairly clever fellow. But here is his uncle showing him a thing or two. And when he complains about the switch, Laban airily replies that it is not the custom in these parts to marry off the younger daughter before the elder. Of course, if Jacob really *wants* Rachel . . . well, he could marry her too. At once, in fact. But it would require another seven years of hard labor.

One can only imagine the cold rage of Jacob. The shrewd dealer had been out-dealt, and there was nothing he could do about it. He could only swallow his anger, serve out his indenture for Rachel, and perhaps one day settle his accounts with Laban.

JACOB SWINDLES LABAN

After many years and many children, Jacob grows restive and decides that it is time to return to his homeland. So he broaches the matter to Laban.

Laban responds to the proposal with alarm. Jacob *go?* His farm has flourished since the arrival of his nephew, now his son-in-law. Jacob is a go-getter. Jacob gets things done. He does not want to see all that ended.

Laban begs Jacob to stay and once more allows him to set his wages. Jacob's request sounds modest enough. He asks for the possession of all the livestock not uniformly colored. Laban agrees, but then, true to form, promptly removes all of the dappled animals in the vicinity.

By now Jacob is beginning to tire of his father-in-law's shenanigans. He retaliates by placing striped sticks near the remaining animals during their breeding. Here we find an old bit of folklore which suggests that visual experiences during conception and gestation will have an effect on the unborn—in this case produce multicolored offspring.

The ploy succeeds. A host of brindled animals appears and soon Jacob finds himself proprietor of the major part of the flocks and herds.

This turn of affairs causes the rift between Jacob and Laban to deepen. Once more Jacob becomes obsessed with the idea that he might have overstayed his welcome. And so, on a day when Laban is conveniently away, Jacob quietly gathers together his wives and servants and flocks, and takes a surreptitious departure, leaving behind an indignant, not to say considerably inpoverished, father-in-law. As if all of this were not enough, Rachel even filches her father's household gods. These idols are not only items of religious veneration (and one catches in the story the amused mockery of the religiously enlightened), but undoubtedly costly objets d'art to boot.

Laban soon hears of Jacob's departure and quickly forms a posse. He catches up with Jacob in Gilead. On this occasion there is little balm. The meeting grows stormy. Charge meets countercharge. But this time Laban gets nowhere with the thoroughly disillusioned and cynical Jacob. Even Laban's attempt to retrieve his household gods fails, since Rachel has cleverly concealed them in the saddle of her camel and sits on them.

A détente between Jacob and Laban is reached. It is sealed with a covenant or agreement—the so-called Mizpah benediction. There are few passages of Scripture so misunderstood as this one. It is widely regarded, and popularly used, as a kind of sanctified farewell. Yet, the true import of the words, "The LORD watch between me and thee, when we are absent one from another," is hardly that. It is rather a clause in a rogues' bargain which requests that the all-seeing Jahweh keep matters straight between two people who cannot trust one another.

JACOB MOLLIFIES ESAU

No sooner has Jacob taken care of the Laban problem than he is faced with that of Esau.

How will his brother be disposed toward him now? Has the passage of years tempered the old recriminations?

The first indications seem ominous. Jacob is told that Esau is coming to meet him in the company of four hundred men. Jacob, we are not surprised to read, becomes "distressed." He is driven to a frenzy of activity. Also, as a sort of last resort, he is driven to prayer.

Deciding to cede a large portion of his recently acquired wealth to Esau as a token of contrition, Jacob shrewdly divides the gift into many parts. Esau will be confronted with the gifts of one small herd of livestock after another, each from "your servant Jacob" to "my lord Esau." In this way, Jacob calculates, any lingering wrath on his brother's part will gradually be placated.

As a final precaution, Jacob puts his entire caravan, including wives and children, on Esau's side of the river. He himself remains alone on the far bank. One must assume that Jacob told himself that if there was to be a general pogrom, he, at least, would be the last to go.

A cowardly tactic? Of course! The Bible never implies otherwise. And yet despite his craven actions, an adversary other than his brother is soon going to force Jacob to become courageous.

On the wilderness side of the river, alone and frightened, Jacob again undergoes a profound religious experience. For him despair turns to panic when a dark figure emerges from the shadows and clutches him in a death grip. Jacob fights back in desperation. The two wrestle through the long cold Syrian night.

As dawn touches the eastern horizon, the dark stranger attempts to break off the battle. Jacob, however, refuses to release him. He clings to his opponent even though his thighbone has been painfully wrenched from the hip socket. At length he wins a grudging blessing from the antagonist. With the blessing comes Jacob's recognition that his dark and bitter struggle has been with none other than God himself.

His name now becomes "Israel," or "he who strives with God"—an appropriate name not only for Jacob, but for his descendants to come.

No person who has struggled for his faith can fail to discern the rich mystical implications of this part of Jacob's story. No one who has encountered God as the dark adversary who lingers at the edges of loneliness and fears and despair will have any difficulty appreciating the timeless story of Jacob's midnight encounter.

The reunion with Esau is anti-climactic. The generous, easy-going elder twin is delighted to see his brother. The description of the reunion is reminiscent of the story of the Prodigal Son.

> Esau ran to meet him and embraced him;
> he threw his arms round him and kissed him,
> and they wept.
>
> —Genesis 33:4

REUBEN DECEIVES JACOB

Back in his homeland Jacob once more renews his covenant with Jahweh. At a certain place his household buries all the old gods and religious articles and pledges a collective loyalty to God. God's part of the bargain is the promise that Jacob will become the father of a great nation.

> And God said to him:
> "I am God Almighty,
> Be fruitful and increase as a nation;
> a host of nations shall come from you,
> and kings shall spring from your body.
> The land which I gave to Abraham and Isaac I give to you;
> and to your descendants after you I give this land."
>
> —Genesis 35:11–12

Jacob takes up residence in Schechem and sets about the
rearing of his twelve sons. Unfortunately, Jacob has not
learned the lessons of parental favoritism. The same mistakes
in upbringing which had influenced him into becoming a
rogue and a cheat are now perpetrated by Jacob upon his
own children. He becomes an example of the dictum that
those who do not learn from the mistakes of history are
doomed to make the same mistakes themselves. Jacob, in
short, begins to display a pronounced affinity for the children
of Rachel, especially Joseph her firstborn.

The stories of Joseph's coat and his slightly megalomanic
dreams are well-known. The reader will doubtless recall the
selling of Joseph into slavery by his brothers. There are few
more poignant scenes in the Bible than that of Jacob's sons
displaying the symbol of their jealousy, the long-sleeved and
now blood-smeared coat, to their father, along with the false-
hood that Joseph had been killed by a wild animal.

The deception was cruel and callous. And yet who can
avoid the elemental justice involved? For was not the pref-
erential treatment of Joseph and the consequent denigration
of his brothers also cruel and callous? Indeed, the deceit is
altogether understandable. To the perceptive reader of the
Bible, the psychological element of the punishment of the
father is never far away in the story of Jacob's relationship
to his ten older sons.

For Jacob the chickens have now come home to roost.
The deceiver, the swindler, the rogue, becomes the pathetic
victim of a particularly heartless bit of dupery. All attempts
to "comfort" him fail. Jacob vows that:

"I will go to my grave mourning for my son."

—Genesis 37:35

But Joseph is to provide the other great surprise in Jacob's
life. For it is not down to his grave, but rather down to

Egypt that Jacob will go to see his favorite son. And in the excitement of that reunion, the covenanted promise of God is renewed once more.

> God said
> "I am God, the God of your father. Do not be afraid to go down to Egypt, for there I will make you a great nation. I will go down with you to Egypt, and I myself will bring you back again without fail; and Joseph shall close your eyes."
>
> —Genesis 46:3–4

Seventeen years would Jacob live in Egypt, separated from the land he cheated his brother to obtain. And while he himself would be buried in Canaan, his descendants would not leave Egypt until they had undergone great persecution and gained their freedom under the leadership of a man named Moses.

In reconsidering the story of Jacob, there is so much to be learned about the character of the Bible that one scarce knows where to begin. Possibly the best place is where we began—with the candor of the Biblical writers and editors. One cannot help but wonder why they showed no reluctance to present the worst sides of the heroes of their religion. Why are we presented with a drunken Noah, or an ill-tempered Moses, or a skeptical Gideon, or a lecherous David, or a roguish Jacob?

Might it not be because there were no heroes for the men who composed the Bible? Might it not be because there was for them only *a* hero—*one* hero, and that was the Lord God. All the rest were fragile men and women. And it was a part of God's heroic greatness that he could use such as these. *Even* the fragments and the flaws of human lives, they realized, somehow had a way of serving the purposes of God and accomplishing his objectives.

Interestingly, the tradition has persisted. There has always been an element in the Church which has resisted the tempting illusions of hagiolatry (the making and veneration of saintly heroes). Those unbelievably virtuous saints of pious imagination always pose a threat. For they tend to replace one's faith in the transforming capacities of God with a faith in the goodness of man. A hollow faith! Man, even at his best, has a way of fumbling things. *Only* God is good, Christ affirmed, and he neatly summed up the magnificent Old Testament doctrines of God and man and the relationship between the two.

Thus Jacob was a rogue. So be it. So are we all at times. Yet Jacob was God's rogue. And his story inspires us to hope that even our mistakes and follies may be transformed by the alchemy of God's providence into the good which God wills for all men.

III GIDEON:
ON FACING ONE'S ENEMIES

It shall not be said, when this victory over Midian is won, that
it was won by Gideon or any other general. This victory shall
be mine. It shall be a miracle. It shall be clear to all Israel
that only the hand of God delivered them.

—*Gideon,* Paddy Chayefsky

A camel, according to the light-hearted definition, is a
horse put together by a committee. We are inclined to be
amused by the *camelus dromedarius,* which is not only a
strange looking beast, but is strange in every respect. It is an
evolutionary freak, preserved from extinction by its adapt-
ability to the waste areas of the globe and its ability to
survive under the most adverse climatic conditions.

It is perhaps the most unloved and unloving of all
man's companion animals, a condition due in part to its
lackluster and somewhat malevolent personality. Too unintelligent to be trained in the true sense of the term,
the Arabian camel is goaded into service every morning
as if for the first time in its life. And every evening it
reverts into indolent wildness.

And yet, for all of its stupidity, for all of its ghastly
shapelessness, the camel has had an immeasurable influence
on the course of human history. Its passive, ill-humored

subservience to those who inhabited the so-called "cradle
of civilization" was a critical factor in any number of economic, military and cultural developments. Indeed, so important was the camel in the shaping of Mediterranean
civilization that it could well be said that in everything
except appearance the camel was no laughing matter.

It was toward the end of the Bronze Age, some twelve
or thirteen hundred years before the time of Christ, that
certain nomads who lived in the Arabian peninsula made
two discoveries about the camel. One was that it could be
prodded and beaten into serving as a beast of burden.

The second discovery was related to the first; namely,
that there was no better form of desert transportation. The
camel's splayed feet were perfectly suited to the desert
sands. Its compartmentalized stomach stored great quantities
of food and water which were passed into its system as needed.
The result was that the beast could cover in excess of twenty-
five miles per day, carry up to a thousand-pound load, and go
nearly half a week without food or water.

Unfortunately, in accordance with one of the sorrier traditions in the history of mankind, the persons who made
these discoveries about the camel did not use their new-
found knowledge to benefit their fellow men. On the contrary, they used it to take advantage of them.

The Midianites, who lived in the Sinai wastes and were
among the first to domesticate the camel, discovered very
quickly that this creature provided efficient transportation
for foraging raids across the Jordan into the agricultural
regions of Israel.

As time went on, these raids became something of a
tradition with the Midianites. With the help of the camel,
the harvests of Israel were theirs for the taking. At the end
of each growing season they would dash westward into the
croplands of Israel, force the hard-working farmers to yield

up their produce, then retire back into the land of Midian to await another harvest.

The Israelites had no way of defending themselves against the blitzkrieg tactics of these camel-mounted warriors. Localized defense seemed impossible, for there was no way of knowing where the highly mobile enemy would strike next. A general defense of the territory seemed equally impossible, for there was neither sufficient time nor numbers of men.

There was nothing to do, therefore, but suffer the periodic depredations of these Bedouins and hope that the next time it would be your neighbor's turn, and not your own, to be visited by them.

Since they were unchecked by Israel, the Midianites grew bolder. Their raiding parties developed into yearly mass migrations into the farmlands of Israel. They came en masse, families and all. They set up huge encampments from which patrols would be sent out to scour the countryside for food. These regular arrivals reminded the Israelites of a plague of locusts; and the Midianites departed in character, leaving behind a country stripped and desolated.

The Israelites' response to the situation was to cower. There seemed no defense, no means of retaliation. They felt themselves powerless before the agile maneuverings of their predators. All they could do was to hide themselves and their produce in caves, hoping that the foraging Midianites would come across neither.

In better days it had been customary to thresh wheat on a raised platform or hill where the wind could blow away the chaff. No one in his right mind would try to thresh wheat in one of those small, dark caverns where the juice of crushed grapes was bottled in sheep and goat skins.

Yet it is in just such cramped quarters that we first run across Gideon, the man who in time would become one of the greatest "judges" of Israel.

And what was Gideon doing in the "winepress"?

He was threshing wheat. This potential hero was hiding himself and his harvest from the desert raiders, for he too was afraid of the Midianites.

How Gideon was persuaded to turn and face the enemies of Israel, and of the clever manner in which he vanquished them so completely that the term "day of Midian" became synonymous in the Hebrew language with total victory, is the subject of chapters six, seven and eight of the book of Judges.

The story is worth our investigation not only for the interesting nature of its fast-paced events, not only for its account of how one man grew resolute in the face of immense odds, but also because of the many insights it provides into Israel's conception of itself and its God.

THEOLOGICAL PRELIMINARIES

Almost all the stories of the Bible, whether found in the Old Testament or the New, are given a theological setting. Mircea Eliade, a foremost authority on primitive religion, has written that men who lived in early times saw literally everything with religious eyes.

This was certainly true of Israel. Every event which took place was assigned a religious meaning. Every account of a historical happening was given a theological interpretation.

Ordinarily, the purpose of this setting was to explain to the listener why Jahweh acted in the way he did. The entire life of Israel was viewed as a series of actions and reactions between Jahweh and his people. If they did such and such, then he did so and so. And so on. Because of it, no story was regarded as complete unless there was some attempt to determine the theological significance of what happened.

The story of Gideon was provided with not one, but *four* theological settings. Each had a definite religious purpose. One explained in religious terms how Midian came to dominate Israel. Two offered more or less miraculous reassurances that in this story it was Jahweh himself who became involved in the crisis. And the last of them reminded the listener that the proper religious response to the intervention of Jahweh was an act of repentance.

Let us be more specific.

The first of these theological settings to the story of Gideon was a religious explanation of how it was that Midian had achieved such an oppressive domination of Israel. To an Israelite of the first millennium before Christ, this was not to be fully accounted for by some chance historical development, such as the domestication of the camel. The military advantage provided by the camel may have been an incidental factor in the troubles of Israel, but the underlying reason for the Midianite oppression was sin. Israel had broken the covenant relationship. The people had turned their allegiance from the true God to false gods. And Jahweh had responded by letting them go, by letting events take their ordinary course. Thus the story of Gideon begins:

The Israelites did what was wrong in the eyes of the Lord, and he delivered them into the hands of Midian for seven years.
—Judges 6:1

The "wrong" in this case refers mainly to the degenerate religious practices associated with the worship of the fertility gods of Canaan, the nature of which will be described elsewhere in this book. To read the Old Testament with any understanding at all, one must recognize its basic theological contention that there is always a causal relationship between purity of religion and integral strength. This is true whether one refers to a nation or an individual. Where religion is right, there is an accompanying and basic invincibility.

Tangent to this axiomatic religious truth is the Old Testament's realistic appraisal of man's constant penchant for bad religion, and the fact that nothing short of the most wrenching adversity will show him the error of his ways.

> And so the Israelites were brought to destitution by the Midianites, and they cried to the LORD for help.
>
> —Judges 6:6

A second theological element prefacing the story of Gideon was intended to assure the listener that the power at work in the events to follow was none other than the God of Israel. In this case an angel of Jahweh (in earlier versions it was no doubt Jahweh himself) appeared to Gideon skulking in his cave and said, "You are a brave man, and the Lord is with you."

Whether this address was meant as something on the order of a sarcastic reproach or, more positively, as a demonstration of Jahweh's capacity to discern the essential character of a man despite all evidences to the contrary, is a minor puzzle which is left to the wit of the reader. What is more pertinent is that here Jahweh intended to invest the latent abilities of Gideon with his own charism.

> "Go and use this strength of yours to free Israel from the power of the Midianites. It is I that send you."
>
> —Judges 6:14

"How can I do that?" Gideon in effect replied. "My clan, the one from which I would be obliged to recruit an army, is the weakest of them all."

The LORD answered, "I will be with you, and you shall lay low all Midian as one man."

—Judges 6:16

Gideon responded by asking for a sign. He wanted what any person in his situation would have wanted—an indication of the reality of the heavenly directive which he had been given. Was this the authentic Jahweh who had spoken to him? Or was it all a delusion, a bit of self-deception, a trick of the imagination, a hallucination?

We read that at this point Gideon left his mysterious visitor and in the true hospitable tradition of that region of the world prepared a meal. When he returned, he was told to place the food on a rock. The strange being then touched the food with his staff, and it disappeared in a puff of fire and smoke.

Gideon responded appropriately. He became afraid. The feat convinced him that it was the awesome Jahweh himself who stood before him. In those days a vision of God was regarded as an omen of imminent death. Gideon, doubtless, was certain that he was about to perish. For this reason he was immediately reassured by the angel: "Do not be afraid, you shall not die."

A third element, by which the story was given theological underpinnings, reminded the listener of the proper response to Jahweh's visitation. When one was granted a religious experience of some sort—a vision of God, the hearing of his voice, an awareness of his presence—there should follow an act of repentance. The only appropriate response to such an awesome occurrence was setting one's religion straight. The self-disclosure of God was to be met with renewed loyalty and allegiance and commitment.

Gideon's repentance took the form of a religious purgation. With the help of some friends, he pulled down the

altar and sacred pole erected by his father in homage to
Baal.

At this point we might pause a moment to deal with a
question which may have occurred to many a reader of the
book of Judges. Namely, what was Gideon's father, an
Israelite, supposedly a worshipper of Jahweh, and even
named in his honor (Joash, "Jahweh gives"), doing with
a shrine dedicated to Baal?

There are several answers which have been proposed. But
the only one which makes much sense is that the man
must have been an apostate. Originally possessed of true
religion, he must have turned at some time in his life to the
worship of Baal.

This likely explanation, incidentally, may account for Gideon's alternate name in the story, Jerubbaal. This particular
name honored Baal ("Baal pleads") and was surely given
to Gideon at birth by his apostate father.

To be sure, the story suggests that the name Jerubbaal
was only given later as a result of Gideon's destruction of the
local altar to Baal. According to this explanation, his action
angered the citizenry; but when they voiced their objections
to Gideon's father, Joash is reputed to have replied, "Let
Baal see to [plead] his own problems." Hence the name
Jerubbaal.

This story, however, sounds a little forced. Hence it seems
not unreasonable to assume that Jerubbaal was the original
name, and Gideon ("hewer" or "grim warrior") something
of an honorary nickname given after the defeat of the Mid-
ians.*

To return to the matter of the story's theological settings,
we come now to the fourth. This, once more, amounts to a
demonstrative proof that it was really Jahweh, and no one
else, who acted in the Midianite crisis. The foil for this

* Some scholars have concluded that the story in the Bible is based on
the exploits of two heroes with these respective names.

proof is Gideon's lingering skepticism. Despite the angelic
visitation, Gideon apparently remained dubious about the
enterprise which Jahweh placed in his hands. He may have
wondered if God really spoke so familiarly to men. He
may have questioned if it were truly God who had in-
vested him with this cause.

The result was Gideon's hankering for further proof not
only of Jahweh's reality, but of his power. Gideon was a
"doubting Thomas," and while the Bible is filled with criticisms of those who ask for signs, and makes the testing
of God a very serious offense indeed, there also seems to
be—as we find in the cases of both Gideon and St. Thomas
—a certain divine patience with those of an extremely skeptical turn of mind.

The well-known incident which followed, the laying out of
the fleece, has about it the hesitancy and uncertainty of any
person who has ever tried to know and to do the will of
God.

> If thou wilt deliver Israel through me as thou hast promised—
> now, look, I am putting a fleece of wool on the threshing-floor.
> If there is dew only on the fleece and all the ground is dry,
> then I shall be sure that thou wilt deliver Israel through me,
> as thou hast promised.
>
> —Judges 6:37

The next morning it was just as he asked. In fact, Gideon
wrung a bowlful of water from the fleece, while the ground
around had remained perfectly dry.

But was Gideon satisfied? Of course not. That's the trouble with bargaining with God. One successful instance leads
to another. One answered demand for religious certainty
draws forth yet another until one would, if one could, make
a virtual slave of God.

The next night Gideon wanted the process reversed. And

the following morning—sure enough! This time the fleece was
dry, while the ground around it was wet. In this manner
Gideon was assured that it was truly Jahweh who was
ordering him into battle with the hosts of Midian.

These, then, are the four theological settings to the story
of Gideon. Only after a religious explanation for the Midianite crisis, only after the reassurance that it was indeed
Jahweh who had personally taken charge of matters, only
after a reminder of the proper response to Jahweh's self-
manifestation do we come to the more historical aspects of
Gideon's career. Only after the religious background is complete is the reader taken to the Valley of Jezreel where
the real action takes place.

GIDEON'S RUSE

As this story opens, we find the Midianites encamped
along a flat and highly accessible stretch of ground known
as the Valley of Jezreel. From here foraging raids were
sent out in all directions. The encampment was the hub of
the invasion strategy.

From a military point of view, the placement was poor.
The Midianites were surrounded on three sides by high
ground from which any potential enemy could both spy
and launch attacks. And yet, there were no practical alternatives available to the Midianites. Camels were more or
less restricted to level terrain and, except for the Valley
of Jezreel, this part of Israel was quite rugged.

At the same time, the Midianites had presumably grown
careless with their military strategy. They no doubt took
their supremacy over the Israelites for granted. They felt
that they could plunder Israel without fear of reprisal.

On this occasion, however, the Midianites were wrong.
Eight miles south of their encampment, Gideon had as-

sembled an army of thirty-two thousand men from the
various tribes of Israel. By contrast to the Midianites, Gideon
had selected his assembly point wisely. A range of high
ground concealed his forces from the Midianite outposts.
To his rear lay mountainous terrain into which his army
could easily retreat in the event of a military reverse.
There, they could be sure, the camels of Midian would not
go.

One can almost imagine Gideon on this occasion sizing
up his army and, quite possibly, feeling some small degree
of optimism. Thirty-two thousand men, after all, amounts
to quite a sizable army. Perhaps, Gideon told himself, Jahweh
was about to make good his promise of victory. But if
not, he had covered his military and religious bets with a
good escape route.

If Gideon entertained such sanguine hopes, they were
soon dispelled. Before attacking the Midianites, or so the
story goes, Gideon was informed by Jahweh that the army
he had assembled was much too large. It would have to
be pared down.

His army too large? Considering the hugeness of the
Midianite force? What kind of talk was this? What possibly could Jahweh have in mind? No doubt Gideon told
God a thing or two, as humans are occasionally prone
to do.

"But consider, Gideon," Jahweh may have argued. "Isn't
it possible for armies to be *too* large? Aren't massive armies
also unwieldy armies? Isn't a small, disciplined, well-organ-
ized force to be preferred to large masses of men with all
of their tendencies toward confusion and chaos?"

Whatever the nature of Jahweh's contention, whatever Gideon's estimate of it, Gideon nevertheless obeyed the orders
of his commander. He summoned his troops and announced
that any person who was in any way reluctant to fight the
Midianites could return home immediately.

For much of the army this offer was almost too good to be
believed. This outfit they were preparing to fight: it wasn't
some irregular force, some ragged, ill-equipped collection of
military greenhorns! Quite the contrary! This was the Grand
Army of Midian, made up of those swaggering bullies from
the east who had been grinding their faces into the dirt
for more years than anyone cared to remember! Who in his
right mind wanted to tackle *these* invincible brutes? The
only reason that any Israelites at all were around is that
they had been forced, conscripted, shamed, railroaded into
Gideon's civilian army. And now, here was their commanding
officer offering a general discharge!

The result was that twenty-two thousand realists promptly
went home.

Gideon must have been utterly dismayed as he surveyed
his diminished army. He may well have counted on considerably more morale in the ranks than that exhibited by
those twenty-two thousand recruits who broke ranks with a
joyous shout and melted into the hills before Gideon could
change his mind.

Here he was now, left with a mere ten thousand men,
and ill-equipped ones at that! What could *they* do against
the camel panzers of Midian?

Perhaps it was in the midst of some rather bitter com-
plaining that Gideon received an additional communique
from on high. This one proved to be more incredible than
the last!

The LORD then said to Gideon, "There are still too many.
Bring them down to the water, and I will separate them for
you there. When I say to you, 'This man shall go with you,'
he shall go; and if I say, 'This man shall not go with you,'
he shall not go." So Gideon brought the people down to the
water and the LORD said to him, "Make every man who laps
the water with his tongue like a dog stand on one side, and on
the other every man who goes down on his knees and drinks."

The number of those who lapped was three hundred, and all the rest went down on their knees to drink, putting their hands to their mouths. The LORD said to Gideon, "With the three hundred men who lapped I will save you and deliver Midian into your hands, and all the rest may go home." So Gideon sent all these Israelites home, but he kept the three hundred, and they took with them the jars and the trumpets which the people had. The Midianite camp was below him in the vale.

—Judges 7:4–8

Whether or not there was any moral significance to this drinking test is not entirely clear. Sunday school children are generally told that this was some sort of examination for vigilance on the part of the soldiers. But we cannot be certain. Conceivably, the action had a meaning which was clear to those who first told and retold the story of Gideon, but was later lost.

Whatever its significance, two results were ever so clear. One was that Gideon had been left with only three hundred men; and the other was that if there were to be any victory against the Midianites, only Jahweh could provide it. After a test of these odds, no one could claim otherwise!

Equipped with the remnants of an army, just three companies of one hundred men each, Gideon was left with the problem of how to engage in battle with the Midianites. Indicative of his basic shrewdness, Gideon turned to military intelligence. We read that with his servant Purah, he set out by night to spy out the Midianite stronghold.

What is interesting about the description of Gideon's investigation of the enemy position is not so much the account of the dream he overheard, but rather the relative ease with which he accomplished his mission. How was Gideon able to infiltrate the enemy's lines so easily? What was undoubtedly a barren and treeless area (as it so remains

L.I.F.E. College Library
1100 Glendale Blvd.
Los Angeles, Calif. 90026

today) offered little opportunity for concealment either by
day *or* night.

One possibility suggests itself; namely, that Gideon and
Purah disguised themselves as Midianites and brazenly
strolled into the enemy encampment. How could they do
this? Because the very crowded condition of the camp made
it nearly impossible to tell friend from foe.

> Now the Midianites, the Amalekites, and the eastern tribes
> were so many that they lay there in the valley like a swarm
> of locusts; there was no counting their camels; in number they
> were like grains of sand on the seashore.
>
> —Judges 7:12

The dream which Gideon heard related by one enemy
soldier to another indicates that the Midianites were aware
of Gideon's insurgent force. How seriously they regarded the
threat is open to debate.

According to the book of Judges, this dream together with
its interpretation emboldened Gideon to attack. And yet it
must have been the potential chaos of the crowded Midianite
campsite which provided Gideon with his basic strategy.

Gideon's plan was more a ruse than anything else. His
idea was to surround the Midianites on three sides with his
three hundred men. Each man would be equipped with a
hooded torch and a ram's horn trumpet (or *shophar*, the
sound of which resembles an unmuffled French horn). At
a signal the torches would flare out, the trumpets blare,
and the men give a mighty shout.

Gideon reasoned that the Midianites could be deceived
into thinking that his small force was but the vanguard of a
much larger army. Each of the three hundred would be
mistaken as a "point," which is to say the first man of a larger
contingent of soldiers.

In their confusion and fear at being awakened from sound sleep by the noise of battle, faced with the prospect of being overrun by three hundred companies, or even battalions, the Midianites would be driven into a panic. They would act accordingly, and be defeated not so much by the forces of Israel as the more terrible and deadly forces of chaos.

More than anything else, the ruse depended on split second timing. Torches could not appear one by one lest the detection of one lonely torch-bearer give away the trick. To prevent this possibility, Gideon had every man conceal his torch in a clay pitcher or jar. Only after the signal was given would the pitchers be broken and the torches flashed out into the night.

To his basic strategy, Gideon added one further refinement. His finishing touch was this: the attack would be made to coincide with the changing of the Midianite guard. Gideon must have felt that the guards would be mistaken in the dark for Israelites and be struck down. The guards, in turn, might suppose that their attackers were also Israelites who had somehow managed to infiltrate the lines. In the resulting confusion, men would begin striking out at every shadowy figure who came near them. In the end they would try to escape and hack their way, if necessary, through the seething mass around them in order to reach the safety of the trans-Jordan.

Gideon and the hundred men who were with him reached the outskirts of the camp at the beginning of the middle watch; the sentries had just been posted. They blew their trumpets and smashed their jars. The three companies all blew their trumpets and smashed their jars, then grasped the torches in their left hands and the trumpets in their right, and shouted, "A sword for the Lord and for Gideon!" Every man stood where he was, all round the camp, and the whole camp leapt up in a panic

and fled. The three hundred blew their trumpets, and throughout the camp the LORD set every man against his neighbour.

—Judges 7:19–22

JUDGE AND JUDGMENT

In his play *Gideon*, Paddy Chayefsky has depicted his
hero as being a rather simple-minded individual who somehow became entangled in a situation which he could never
quite comprehend. The witless Gideon of the play is a
charming dramatic figure. But he bears little resemblance
to the Biblical Gideon. The Gideon of the book of Judges
was a man of immense intelligence and will.

Lest this be doubted, lest it be assumed that Gideon's
tactical ruse was nothing more than a lucky chance, let the
reader be reminded of the victory's aftermath. A man of
lesser ability would have been content with the rout at
Jezreel. Gideon, by contrast, proved to be content with
nothing less than a complete victory.

One recurring mistake commonly found among military
commanders is their failure to follow up victory on the
battlefield with the pursuit and destruction of the opposing
army. Many students of the Civil War, for example, feel that
Meade's failure to follow up the Northern victory at Gettys-
burg, by allowing the Army of Northern Virginia to retreat
unmolested into the Cumberland, was a serious error in
military judgment which had the effect of prolonging the
war by months, if not years.

Such was not the case with Gideon. Having routed the
Midianites from Israel, he then set about the systematic
destruction of their retreating armies. Gideon must have
realized that such a procedure would be necessary if the
war were to be fully won. He understood that a routed

army was not necessarily a defeated one. The scattered elements can regroup. They can come back and fight another day.

Because Gideon understood this, he did not rest until the forces of Midian had been totally destroyed and its leaders caught and punished.

Interestingly, the battle in the Valley of Jezreel was probably the easiest part of the campaign against Midian. It was the ensuing pursuit which was truly difficult. Gideon pushed his men mercilessly after the retreating enemy. He made them trek through the bleak desert terrain east of the Jordan, battling stragglers all the way. From all indications, he would not let them rest. Despite hunger and thirst, the Israelites kept up their pursuit of the enemy. Even discouragement, as when their kinsmen in Succoth and Penuel refused to provide them with food, failed to stop Gideon and his loyal troops.

In the end they succeeded. There came at last the total victory they sought.

> Thus the Midianites were subdued by the Israelites; they could no longer hold up their heads. For forty years the land was at peace, all the lifetime of Gideon, that is Jerubbaal son of Joash; and he retired to his own home.
>
> —Judges 8:28–29

We read that after the war Gideon took certain spoils. The most advantageous of them, however, he refused. When asked to become king of Israel, Gideon declined. His reason? As there was but one victor at Jezreel—Jahweh—so there could be only one king of Israel.

> "I will not rule over you, nor shall my son; the LORD will rule over you."
>
> —Judges 8:23

And so Gideon retired with his laurels and lived to a "ripe old age."

But what of Israel? Having cried to Jahweh for deliverance from Midian, did they respond to their deliverance with a lasting revival of true religion?

Not exactly. Israel could never seem to get things straight. It was the old story, repeated again and again throughout that dolorous yet splendid history:

"They forgot the LORD their God who had delivered them from their enemies on every side . . ."

—Judges 8:34

Despite having been granted a victory over Midian, despite a long period of relative prosperity, Israel soon returned to its old pagan ways. The religious revival cooled. The old immorality put in its enticing appearance and was welcomed as the latest cultural innovation. The worship of Baal became chic. There may have even been a "Death of Jahweh" movement.

The results were predictable. There came a consequent weakness. The nation grew flaccid and ignorant. The people lost all ability to perceive the real dangers which faced them. In time they even lost the ability to defend themselves.

Unfortunately, then, there is no happily-ever-after ending to the story of Gideon. Under his leadership the people won a war. But apparently they learned nothing from it. Nor did they lose time in forgetting the God who gave them the victory.

Charles de Gaulle once said that every defeat contains the seeds of victory, and every victory the seeds of defeat. The importance seems to lie in the ability to distinguish the two varieties of seeds and to act accordingly.

This is something which Israel seemed unable to do. And, to be honest about it, few nations since have done better.

The trouble with Gideon's total victory was its brevity. It didn't last. The sad conclusion of the story of his absolute devastation of the Midianites—one as total as the destruction of Japan and Germany during World War II—is contained in the pages which follow the story of Gideon.

Once more the Israelites did what was wrong in the eyes of the LORD, worshipping the Baalim and the Ashtaroth, the deities of Aram and of Sidon and of Moab, of the Ammonites and of the Philistines. They forsook the LORD and did not worship him. The LORD was angry with Israel, and he sold them to the Philistines and the Ammonites, who for eighteen years harassed and oppressed the Israelites who lived beyond the Jordan in the Amorite country in Gilead. Then the Ammonites crossed the Jordan to attack Judah, Benjamin, and Ephraim, so that Israel was in great distress. The Israelites cried to the LORD for help and said, "We have sinned against thee; we have forsaken our God and worshipped the Baalim." And the LORD said to the Israelites, "The Egyptians, the Amorites, the Ammonites, the Philistines; the Sidonians too and the Amalekites and the Midianites—all these oppressed you and you cried to me for help; and did not I deliver you? But you forsook me and worshipped other gods; therefore I will deliver you no more. Go and cry for help to the gods you have chosen, and let them save you in the day of your distress." But the Israelites said to the LORD, "We have sinned. Deal with us as thou wilt; only save us this day, we implore thee." They banished the foreign gods and worshipped the LORD; and he could endure no longer to see the plight of Israel.

—Judges 10:6–16

IV SAUL:
A BIBLICAL TRAGEDY

For God's sake, let us sit upon the ground
And tell sad stories of the death of kings:
How some have been depos'd; some slain in war;
Some haunted by the ghosts they have depos'd;
Some poison'd by their wives; some sleeping killed;
All murder'd: for within the hollow crown
That rounds the mortal temples of a king
Keeps Death his court, and there the antic sits,
Scoffing his state and grinning at his pomp,
Allowing him a breath, a little scene,
To monarchize, be fear'd, and kill with looks,
Infusing him with self and vain conceit,
As if this flesh which walls about our life
Were brass impregnable; and humour'd thus
Comes at the last and with a little pin
Bores through his castle wall, and—farewell king!

—Richard II

He was like a falling star. Men were dazzled by his brief,
fiery career. It burned brightly against the friction of his
times. But it was a descent most of the way.

He emerged from relatively obscure origins. He mustered

the first significant resistance to his country's enemies in a generation, and a grateful people acclaimed him king. He continued to check the Philistines, the greatest of Israel's opponents—even drove them back. At the same time he tamed some of the more currish border enemies which snapped at the heels of the twelve tribes.

He was a brilliant, valiant man, but also one whose mental balance was a bit precarious. He did not, however, allow his occasional "spells" to interfere with his goals. In a remarkably short time he accomplished what no one since Joshua had been able to do; namely, to weld the majority of the federated tribes of Israel into a cohesive political unit.

Militarily, he was the greatest of his times. He seems to have been one of those rare generals who combine an imaginative, unorthodox and shrewd sense of tactics with an astonishing grasp of grand strategy.

Yet he made the mistake of arousing the enmity of two of the most beloved of Old Testament figures—David, the man who would succeed him to the throne, and Samuel the prophet. Accordingly, he would be remembered largely for his murderous hatred of the one, and his fruitless devotion to the other—a devotion which was sparsely returned at first; later not at all.

He managed to make himself the butt of that moralism which is dinned into the ears of children: "To obey is better than sacrifice," and this together with the other odds and ends of his ill fortune, caused posterity to regard him somewhat negatively.

Despite this, Saul, the son of Kish and the first king of Israel, was a better man than most people suspect. Indeed, he may have been a person vastly superior to Samuel, his religious alter ego, and even his successful rival David.

Impossible? Not entirely. A careful reading of the Scriptures can lead to some rather surprising conclusions.

What kind of person was King Saul? How did he manage
to become king? What sort of reign did he exercise? Why
did he eventually harbor such a hatred for David? And why
was his kingship rejected by Samuel, the man who had
originally anointed him?

THE RIDDLE OF I SAMUEL

In order to answer these questions, it is necessary first of
all to take a close look at the sources of our information
about Saul. These are contained in the first book of Samuel.

Few books of the Bible are so baffling as I Samuel. Not
that it does not read easily. It does. No one need struggle
to grasp the meaning in its thirty-one fast-paced chapters.

And yet one can hardly avoid the contradictions which
fill its pages—contradictions in fact, contradictions in outlook.

I Samuel constitutes something of a standing reproach to
those who would have the Bible an oracle broadcast verbatim
from the porches of heaven. Which is not, by the way, to
say that we are obliged to rule out the divine inspiration
of the book. Rather, we are pressed to ponder the manner
in which the Holy Spirit sometimes operates. After all, God
moves in a mysterious way, as the hymnodist put it.

I Samuel reinforces an insight of P. T. Forsyth, that remarkable prophet of an earlier part of our century. Forsyth,
a rather conservative theologian in many respects, was nevertheless highly enthusiastic about Biblical scholarship. He
would often say that the Holy Spirit was as operative in
the minds of Biblical scholars as in the hearts of the original
writers.

The possibility that the so-called "higher critics" were
inspired by the Holy Spirit is an idea which might grate on
the nerves of many a "Bible-believing Christian." But who

would dare rule out the possibility? Or deny that honest Biblical investigation has helped in the case under discussion?

For example, the scholarship of the past century has enabled us to understand that the inconsistencies of I Samuel have an understandable origin. It has shown, among other things, that this particular portion of the Bible is a composite. I Samuel was pieced together from several sources, and pieced together in a way which did not entirely resolve the source disagreements.

How did this happen?

Let us suppose that we have been transported back in time to a period in Israel's life some five and one-half centuries before the time of Christ. At the moment we are taking a tour of one of the nation's religious sanctuaries. Suddenly we chance upon a group of priest-scholars laboring over a pile of scrolls.

"And what are they doing?" we might ask our guide.

"They are putting together a history of Israel," he replies. "The scrolls you see contain the information that will go into the history."

"Where do the scrolls come from?"

"From the north, mainly. But in reality from all over— both Israel and Judah."

Anticipating the next question, the guide goes on, "As you can see, some of these scrolls are very old. That brown specimen over there is at least five hundred years old. It cracks easily, so these men are very particular about it. Other scrolls are quite a bit newer."

One of our group asks, "What procedure do they follow? I mean, are they writing this history fresh? Or are they simply arranging these materials in chronological order and allowing them to speak for themselves?"

"Actually," says the guide, who suspects this fellow of being a quibbler, "they're doing a bit of both, though con-

centrating on the latter technique. They want these old
documents to speak for themselves. That means that they
will try to piece them together in a chronological fashion.
But since these sources are so varied in time and in form
—why, we have biography here, and history, and poems, and
sagas, and laws, and sermons, and all sorts of things!—
it will be necessary for them to flesh out these materials
with a bit of their own writing. Does that answer your
question?"

Not completely, the questioner tells himself, though he
nods affirmatively. Rather than ask the guide any further
questions, he silently vows to check into the matter the
minute he can get hold of a good introduction to the Bible.

In working upon that part of Israel's history which had to
do with the establishment of the monarchy, these Deuteronomic editors (as they are now called) were faced with a
peculiar difficulty. It was simply that the two major documents on the subject held contrary views on the matter of
the *need* for a monarchy in Israel. One felt that it was both
necessary and divinely ordained. The other regarded it as an
apostasy.

Imagine the problems which this source conflict must have
generated! It would be as though a scholar today attempted
to write a history of the American Revolution with but two
sources of information, one of which fashioned events in favor
of the British Crown, while the other used only that data
which supported the position of the American Separatists.

The more recent of the two basic sources of I Samuel
(by nearly three hundred years) appears to have been a
popular biography of the prophet Samuel. Underlying its
evident veneration of this religious figure, however, there
lurked another theme: namely, an indictment of the institution of monarchy. The truth of it is that this piece of
literature was something of a political tract. The bias of the
writer shows through at many points. One can detect through-

out a deep bitterness over the conduct of the kings of Israel and Judah together with the plea that there be a return to the system of judges, the political structure which originally held the twelve tribes together in a loose confederation.

This form of government, according to the author, was what God meant for Israel. Not kings! Not monarchs! God alone was king! Only Jahweh was meant to reign over the children of Israel! To subscribe to any regent but God could only be regarded as a form of idolatry! Consequently, the establishment of the monarchy under Saul was clearly no gift of God. Rather it was a punishment visited upon his disobedient people.

Accordingly, Samuel, the last of the judges of Israel, appears in this document as an angry man of God who desperately attempts to stave off the institution of monarchy. Saul, by contrast, does not show up so well.

The following passage from I Samuel illustrates the attitude to be found in the later source toward the monarchy:

But their request for a king to govern them displeased Samuel, and he prayed to the LORD. The LORD answered Samuel, "Listen to the people and all that they are saying; they have not rejected you, it is I whom they have rejected, I whom they will not have to be their king. They are now doing to you just what they have done to me since I brought them up from Egypt: they have forsaken me and worshipped other gods . . ."

—I Samuel 8:6–8

Compare this with the approach found in the earlier source. Here the beginnings of royal rule are viewed as a directive from God. The calling of Saul, in fact, in some measure resembles that of Moses.

Now the day before Saul came, the LORD had disclosed his intention to Samuel in these words: "At this same time tomorrow

I will send you a man from the land of Benjamin. Anoint him
prince over my people Israel, and then he shall deliver my
people from the Philistines. I have seen the sufferings of my
people and their cry has reached my ears."

—I Samuel 9:15–16

According to the author of the early source, monarchy
had become an inevitability for Israel. Circumstances demanded it. Only under the guidance of a central ruler
could the twelve tribes unite effectively against their pestilent
enemies. No longer was the tribal system able to provide
a common defense. Communication between the tribes was
inefficient. Military operations were, at best, haphazard. Only
a combined sovereign and general could secure their borders
against the depredations of the Philistines and others. So,
the author suggests, the people called on God. And God
gave them a king—Saul.

For the editors working on Israel's history, the presence
of two such contrary sources must have caused many late
nights. What to do? Should the divergent materials be placed
in tandem, one after the other?

But this would only confuse things. Israel required a
straightforward account of its political and religious background, not a potpourri of contradictions.

Quite possibly one of the editors suggested that the latter
source, the tract against monarchy, be eliminated altogether.
But the others would have ruled out this solution. These
men felt too great a reverence for *all* of the documents
relating to the history of Israel to allow one to disappear
from view.

There remained but one option: to attempt to combine
these contradictory documents, along with various other fragments, into one single account.

This they did. And the result was I Samuel.

While the inconsistencies resulting from its varied sources have continued to plague readers, it remains a tribute to the skill of these editors that scholars have not been entirely successful in disentangling the elements of this book. The major contradictory sources have proved easy enough. But many of the nuances continue to escape categorization.

In our study of King Saul, we shall depend almost completely on the earlier source. Not only is it more accurate, more objective, and more engaging; it also bears the distinction of being one of the most skillful bits of contemporary history ever written. Scholars universally attest the genius of its author. He combined a magnificent prose style with a profound grasp of the significance of the events which swirled round him. He was able to separate the wheat of history from its chaff. He sensed the significance of the events he described, and yet could adduce fascinating and illuminating detail, as when he put this misinformation into the mouths of Israel's enemies:

When the Ark came into the camp all the Israelites greeted it with a great shout, and the earth rang with the shouting. The Philistines heard the noise and asked, "What is this great shouting in the camp of the Hebrews?" When they knew that the Ark of the LORD had come into the camp, they were afraid and cried, "A god has come into the camp. We are lost! No such thing has ever happened before. We are utterly lost! Who can deliver us from the power of these mighty gods?"
                                                            —I Samuel 4:5–8

Note the error as to the number of gods venerated by the Israelites.

Though some scholars have attempted to pinpoint the author of the early source, we need not pursue their speculations. That he was an eyewitness of at least some of the

events which he described can be safely concluded. His
manuscript was probably completed shortly after King David's
death.

Using, then, this strand of I Samuel, let us trace out the
career of this strange, star-crossed first king of Israel.

UP FROM OBSCURITY

The story of Saul begins with the defeat of Israel by the
Philistines at the battle of Ebenezer.

During this disastrous battle, the Ark of the Covenant
had been captured and carried off to the Philistine temple
of Dagon.

The significance of this loss cannot be overestimated. The
Ark was the most sacred of Israel's cultic objects. It signified
the presence of the Lord of Hosts. In it were to be found
the most cherished mementos of Israel's history.

Now this reliquary had been seized—had, indeed, been
desecrated by being offered to the strange god of an uncircumcised people. At Ebenezer, therefore, military catastrophe had been capped by spiritual catastrophe.

The demoralizing impact of this double disaster upon the
tribes of Israel can only be imagined. Nor was the chain of
misfortune at an end.

Eli, the nearly blind old judge of Israel, upon hearing the
news of the defeat, fell dead, leaving the tribal federation
leaderless. Then, shortly after Eli's death, came a series of
edicts from the Philistines designed to cripple Israel's economy. The worst of them prohibited ironmongering. By it
the Philistines hoped to eliminate the capacity of Israel to
forge arms. No swords, however, meant no plowshares as
well.

In sum, the consequences of the defeat at Ebenezer were

fourfold. Israel had been desolated militarily, politically, economically and religiously. For the tribes it was a time of humiliation and chaos.

Defeat, nevertheless, has its uses. Defeat arouses the processes of self-examination. The vanquished ask why, and not infrequently are granted some very wholesome though painful insights.

In this case, the Israelites must have begun to realize that, among other things, the days of the judges were over. The political patchwork over which the judges of Israel exercised authority—it was the states' rights system of that day—had worked so long as Israel was not seriously challenged from outside.

But such was no longer the case. The Philistines had grown strong and hungry. Other tribes had taken to eyeing choice bits of border real estate. It proved to be a new situation with new problems. And new problems demand new solutions. The flimsy tribal federation, with each tribe jealously maintaining its rights, no longer provided an effective defense. A deeper unity was needed—a unity both practical and symbolic.

Thus, after Ebenezer the question was no longer *would* there be a central ruler; rather the question had already become, *who* would this central ruler be?

In relating the traditional tales about Saul's emergence to prominence, it is helpful to remember that to the Semitic mind of that day, the *unexpected* provided the movement to any good story. It was the sudden turn of events, the coincidences, the unanticipated developments which appealed to the tellers and hearers of Israel's history. Not only did such elements provide the promise of some quirkish happenstance, keeping the listener alert; they also served to remind everyone of the whimsical ways in which the Lord operated.

No power from the east nor from the west,
no power from the wilderness, can raise a man up.
　For God is judge;
he puts one man down and raises up another.

—Psalm 75:6–7

In the situation at hand, the first king of Israel was
vaulted to power while engaging in, of all things, a search
for a herd of lost asses. One can almost hear a nomadic
storyteller by a campfire: ". . . and so if it hadn't been for
those stupid asses wandering off into the canebrake, we
probably never would have heard of Saul, the son of Kish."

Incidentally, the story about Saul and the lost asses served
yet another function. It informed its hearers that Saul was
from a well-to-do background. Anyone who possessed such
a herd to be lost in the first place was clearly a few notches
above average.

At the time his story begins, Saul was probably nearing
the prime of life, somewhere around the age of forty. He
had a family of his own, including a nearly grown son named
Jonathan. Since Saul's father was himself alive, Saul, in the
Semitic tradition, remained an obedient son. This does not
mean, however, as people often assume, that Saul was a
particularly young man when anointed king.

The asses had been lost, and Kish had ordered his son
to look for them. The search, however, proved unsuccessful.

Then the unexpected. As Saul was about to return home
empty-handed, one of his servants suggested that he consult
a local seer, a man who apparently was regarded as something of a clairvoyant. Perhaps *he* could direct them to the
lost asses. Saul quickly agreed.

The seer turned out to be Samuel, successor to Eli. Already apprised by God that the future king of Israel was about
to put in an appearance, Samuel put Saul's query about the

lost animals to one side and concentrated his attention upon
the man whose path he had so unexpectedly crossed.

Saul must have looked regal. He was tall and strong.
There was something compelling about the man. Not at all
arrogant, he was polite, pious and suitably humble.

> The moment Saul appeared the LORD said to Samuel, "Here
> is the man of whom I spoke to you. This man shall rule my
> people." Saul came up to Samuel in the gateway and said,
> "Would you tell me where the seer lives?" Samuel replied, "I
> am the seer. Go on ahead of me to the hill-shrine and you
> shall eat with me today; in the morning I will set you on your
> way, after telling you what you have on your mind. Trouble
> yourself no more about the asses lost three days ago, for they
> have been found. But what is it that all Israel is wanting? It
> is you and your ancestral house." "But I am a Benjamite," said
> Saul, "from the smallest of the tribes of Israel, and my family
> is the least important of all the families of the tribe of Ben-
> jamin. Why do you say this to me?"
>
> —I Samuel 9:17–21

There may have been something else about Saul which
impressed Samuel. Let us hazard the conjecture that there
may have been that indefinable character within the eyes,
that look which signifies genius and vision and the capacity
for religious ecstasy—all of which Saul possessed in good
measure. Such a look to the eyes—and we have all seen it!
—also indicates the possibility of emotional disarray, even
outright insanity. In other words, Samuel may have been able
to detect in Saul what one poet has called a "fertile lack
of balance."

Within a short time of his meeting Saul, all of Samuel's
remaining doubts about his kingly possibilities were dispelled.
As Saul prepared to take his leave, the sacred oil was poured
upon his head, and the prophet recited:

"The LORD anoints you prince over his people Israel; you shall rule the people of the LORD and deliver them from the enemies round about them."

—I Samuel 10:1

THE FIRST KING OF ISRAEL

It is difficult to surmise what may have happened next to Saul. Perhaps he went directly to Gilgal and there engaged in his first falling out with Samuel by assuming the prophet's prerogatives and offering the sacrifice. In order to follow this sequence of events, the reader must skip from chapter ten to thirteen.

The Deuteronomic editors imply, however, that Saul returned to farming. It was, they say, while he was plowing a field that there came the news which would force the self-demeaning Saul to take charge of Israel's destiny—the news of the impending disaster at Jabesh Gilead.

Jabesh Gilead was a city in the trans-Jordan and quite far to the north. Because of its location it was unusually vulnerable, and especially so after the tribes were subdued by the Philistines. The weakened Israelites, particularly those along the border, found themselves harassed and victimized by other traditional enemies, even those hitherto regarded as contemptible.

For Jabesh Gilead, trouble came from the Ammonites, a people in the area who seemed intent on enlarging their terrain at Israel's expense. Under Nahash their leader, the Ammonites put Jabesh Gilead under siege. The besieged Israelites attempted to negotiate. Nahash agreed to settle upon one condition: that the right eyes of the inhabitants of the city be gouged out.

It was a deliberately cruel gesture and a needless one.

Its sole intent was to humiliate, to parade the people of Jabesh Gilead before the world as beggarly weaklings.

It also had, for Nahash, the unfortunate effect of mobilizing the twelve tribes of Israel. The men of Jabesh Gilead pleaded for time. Nahash contemptuously granted a seven-day reprieve, confident that no one would come to their aid.

Shortly afterward, far to the south, Saul learned of the plight of Jabesh Gilead. He became enraged. Grasping a sword, he cut the team of oxen with which he had been plowing into small pieces. These in turn were sent throughout Israel as a summons to battle.

Perhaps by this act Saul meant to demonstrate the power of his sword. Every military leader of those times was expected to be a skillful fighter in his own right. Saul intended to show the strength of his right arm. The Bible also makes it clear that the gesture served as a threat to those Israelites who might have entertained some doubts about going to the defense of their distant cousins.

When Saul heard this, the spirit of God suddenly seized him. In his anger he took a pair of oxen and cut them in pieces, and sent messengers with the pieces all through Israel to proclaim that the same would be done to the oxen of any man who did not follow Saul and Samuel into battle.

—I Samuel 11:6–7

The tribes responded. An army was quickly mustered and the Ammonites were sent scurrying home, tails between legs.

How ecstatic the Israelites must have been with their victory! After all those defeats!

One other thing. How much they were able to accomplish when united! How powerful Israel could really be with a warrior like Saul as leader!

In a delirium of triumph, Saul was carried off to Gilead
and there acclaimed ruler. A new era in Israel had begun.
The era of kings.

THE END OF THE BEGINNING

Saul's reign may have lasted twelve years. We cannot be
certain. All that we can be truly sure of is that his was not
a very pleasant reign. Saul's was one of those situations in
which all the liabilities of power are experienced, but none
of the benefits. Few, certainly, would care to exchange places
with Saul if they knew the truth of it. His life must have
been miserable most of the time. One suspects that he often
wished he were back at the plow, that he had never laid
eyes on Samuel, or heard of Jabesh Gilead, for Saul's days
were filled with warfare and his nights with court intrigue.

When Saul had made his throne secure in Israel, he fought
against his enemies on every side, the Moabites, the Ammonites,
the Edomites, the king of Zobah, and the Philistines; and
wherever he turned he was successful. He displayed his
strength by defeating the Amalekites and freeing Israel from
hostile raids. . . . There was bitter warfare with the Philistines
throughout Saul's lifetime; any strong man and any brave
man that he found he took into his own service.

—I Samuel 14:47–48, 52

Saul had neither the inclination nor the opportunity to
erect royal cities. He did not surround himself with luxury.
His court was far from regal. Archeologists have uncovered
his fortress at Gibeah and found it most unprepossessing.

Saul's home life was exemplary. He had one wife, three
sons and two daughters. There were no Bathsheba-type incidents in Saul's life that we know of. Very likely he could
not find the time to disport himself in this manner.

Besides the endless demands of the battlefield, Saul's life was further burdened by his conflicts with David and Samuel. Even worse were the conflicts spawned deep within his own psyche.

The rift with Samuel was there from the beginning. Invisible, perhaps, but like a hairline crack in fine china, sufficient to render the relationship doubly fragile.

It began at Gilgal where Saul, impatient with Samuel's delay, himself offered the sacrifices which by tradition were reserved to the prophet alone.

Saul's final breach with Samuel, however, occurred under circumstances which cannot help but make the thoughtful student of the Bible ponder. In the midst of his campaigns, Saul was told by Samuel that the Lord had ordered the complete annihilation of a Bedouin tribe to the south of Judah known as the Amalekites.

> Samuel said to Saul, "The LORD sent me to anoint you king over his people Israel. Now listen to the voice of the LORD. This is the very word of the LORD of Hosts: 'I am resolved to punish the Amalekites for what they did to Israel, how they attacked them on their way up from Egypt.' Go now and fall upon the Amalekites and destroy them, and put their property under ban. Spare no one; put them all to death, men and women, children and babes in arms, herds and flocks, camels and asses."
>
> —I Samuel 15:1–3

The Amalekites were detested by Israel for their merciless rapacity, especially as evidenced in the robbery and murder of stragglers during the march through the Wilderness. The grudge had simmered for generations. The book of Deuteronomy reflects the sullen hatred:

> Remember what the Amalekites did to you on your way out of Egypt, how they met you on the road when you were faint

and weary and cut off your rear, which was lagging behind
exhausted: they showed no fear of God. When the LORD your
God gives you peace from your enemies on every side, in the
land which he is giving you to occupy as your patrimony,
you shall not fail to blot out the memory of the Amalekites
from under heaven.

—Deuteronomy 25:17–19

Samuel may have reasoned that Israel was now strong
enough to settle old scores. The time for reprisal had come.

Nevertheless, it is all but impossible for a modern man to
conceive of God conveying such a heartless, vindictive command as this. Nor can we imagine how a man of God like
Samuel could transmit such an order without suspecting that
it was of the devil, not God.

Even the fact that such pogroms were commonplace in
the civilizations of that day does not mitigate the harshness
and ferocity of this supposed divine order. We can only
assume that in many respects the religion of that time was
faulty, that its prophets and priests shared in its errors.
Christ, who opposed the concept of war in general, must
have been horrified by the instances of *herem*, or holy war,
which were a part of his people's history. Implicit in his
teachings is a denial that the loving God whom he called
"Father" could have ordered such bloodthirsty vendettas as
this.

Unaware of any such doctrine of God, but left to the
mercy of Samuel's dogmatic pronouncements, Saul dutifully
trooped his army southward, and there handily dispatched
the Amalekites. Apparently it was not quite the slaughter
prescribed, since the Amalekites appear later on in the book
of Samuel. Still, Saul's army must have wiped out a large
proportion of the tribe.

Contrary to Samuel's orders, however, Saul did not
slaughter all of the livestock. The choicest were reserved for

a sacrificial meal. Nor did he put the Amalekite king, Agag, to the sword.

Upon hearing of Saul's disobedience, Samuel rushed to Gilgal, the scene of an earlier altercation between the prophet and the king, and there bitterly accused Saul of outright insubordination.

Saul defended himself as best he could. One wonders if the thought crossed Saul's mind: "This is a strange way of congratulating a man on a victory."

In any event, Saul did try to explain to Samuel that the livestock was saved not as personal booty, but for sacrifice.

Doubtless Samuel was ready with an answer. He must have known that this was what Saul would say. Obviously the animals were going to be sacrificed. Else why had they been taken to Gilgal?

In stinging words the prophet said to Saul:

> Does the LORD desire offerings and sacrifices
> as he desires obedience?
> Obedience is better than sacrifice,
> and to listen to him than the fat of rams.
>
> —II Samuel 1:19–27

Saul responded meekly. "I have sinned," he confessed. From a Christian perspective one would expect the assurance of divine forgiveness at this. There is no reason to doubt the integrity of Saul's contrition. He felt genuinely sorry for what he had done, and now all that he desired from the prophet was some word of absolution. He would have even done penance.

But Samuel was not to be mollified. He refused to pardon Saul, and in burning phrases informed the king that the Lord had rejected his leadership over Israel.

Saul groveled. We read that he took hold of the skirt of Samuel's robe. When Samuel turned to go, the cloth ripped, providing the prophet with yet another opportunity for denunciation.

Unless one is theologically obliged to accept Samuel's claims of a privileged relationship to God—which, from a Reformation point of view, is quite unacceptable—Samuel himself is judged in this event. We are not attracted by what we see—a man who seems to have used his religious office in an extremely arbitrary manner. One is reminded of the scene of Henry IV, later Holy Roman emperor, kneeling in the snow outside of the palace of Pope Gregory at Canossa, begging that the ban of excommunication be lifted.

It might seem strange to many a reader that anyone would have the temerity to question the character of Samuel, a man so highly regarded in the pages of Scripture. But Samuel was, after all, a man; and not a wholly admirable one at that. He could be rude, self-centered, overbearing. Furthermore, he was often wrong.

Worst of all, there was a streak of fanaticism in Samuel. Consider what happened after he had anathematized Saul. Agag, king of the Amalekites, was commanded to be brought before Samuel. And, we read:

Then Samuel hewed Agag in pieces before the LORD at Gilgal.
—I Samuel 15:33

The words appall. The deed chills. To butcher a helpless prisoner and to make it a religious act demonstrates the extremes to which religious fanaticism all too often lead. One can almost sympathize with one of the second-century heretics, Marcion, who believed that the God depicted in the Old Testament was the evil God of the cosmos, and in no way to be identified with the beneficent God who was the father of Jesus Christ.

And the poignancy of the incident! By this time Agag fully expected to be spared. When summoned by Samuel,

Agag came with some measure of hope for his life, assuring himself, "Surely the bitterness of death has passed."

One cannot read this portion of I Samuel objectively without developing some serious reservations about Samuel. In comparison Saul seems almost an exemplary figure—devout, chaste, valiant and of a deep, almost credulous faith. The faults of the king seem utterly inconsequential.

But what of the prophet? Is it possible to detect in Samuel an irrational hatred for the man who deprived him of so many of his rights as a judge of Israel?

Of one thing we can be sure. Samuel's rejection of Saul and his anointing of David while Saul still occupied the throne played an important part in the tragedy which was to follow.

TWO QUESTIONS

Here we must pass quickly over the account of Saul's turbulent and tangled relationship with David, his young rival. The reader is referred to I Samuel 16 and following. Here he will encounter as exciting reading as can be found in the Bible, especially if one of the newer translations is used. All that is required is a bit of sacred imagination to kindle the adventure of this period of Israel's history.

As the drama gathers momentum, various figures one by one share the stage with the two great antagonists, Saul and David. Each is vividly sketched in by the writer: Jonathan, Michal, Eliab, Abner, Goliath, Abigail, Nabal, Ahimelech and others.

The hairbreadth escapes, the intrigues, the whispered oaths of fealty, the suspense-laden encounters, the exchange of roles as the major figures turn now hunter, now quarry— all add up to adventure of the highest order.

At this point, however, we might restrict our attention

to the posing of two intriguing questions, the first of which has to do with the story of Goliath, and the second the motives of David.

First, *Why did not Saul himself take up the challenge of the giant of Gath, Goliath?*

The reader will recall the circumstances surrounding the slaying of Goliath. The armies of Israel and Philistia faced one another across the valley of Elah. An impasse had been created by the presence of a monstrous soldier who, each day, would approach the Israelite lines and challenge any one of Saul's soldiers to individual combat. Doubtless Goliath was a real bruiser. Scholars estimate his height to have been somewhere in the neighborhood of eight feet, perhaps more.

But when it is recalled that Saul himself was unusually tall, and that he was a man of extraordinary strength (remember that David seems to have been hampered by the sheer weight of Saul's body armor), one is bound to ask why he did not take up the challenge himself. Surely Saul was the logical person to do so, even though he may have been a bit overage. Still I Samuel makes it clear that he remained in fighting shape until his life was abruptly ended at Gilboa. Then why did not Saul take up the challenge of Goliath?

The question points to the story itself. Might there not be more to the story of Goliath than meets the eye? Is it not possible that this fetching tale performs an exceedingly critical function in the account of the monarchy's establishment?

A clue might come from the book of II Samuel where another person by the name of Elhanan is credited with killing Goliath. What this discrepancy might signal is that the story of Goliath has far more than an anecdotal function. Indeed it is quite possible that the story of Goliath might be an astute bit of artistry, the purpose of which was to explain why David deserved the throne.

Here is how it may have been done. Taking a number

of stories about David's youthful valor, together with the well-known story of the victory over Goliath, the author of the early source fashioned a very pointed metaphorical tale. In it the giant represented Philistia in all of its terrifying bulk, defying the armies of the living God. Saul represented the old order in the face of the Philistine threat, while David represented the new.

What the author intended is that his readers realize that there came a point in Saul's life when he lost heart. The Philistines began to terrify him. When this happened, there appeared on the scene a resourceful young man who was not afraid of challenging the Philistine monolith; and not challenging it only, but challenging it with the inferior weaponry which was the lot of the ironless Israelites. By so doing he, David, assumed the right to lead Israel.

This interpretation of the story of Goliath is admittedly speculative. Most readers would probably be content to take the story at face value. In that event the story remains quite plausible as it stands. That David killed a hulking warrior or two is highly possible. The Philistines tended to be rather large anyway, and it does not strain credulity to believe that some of them were immense. Conceivably there might have been more than one of these giants named Goliath. Even then the story is more than a story, for in the encounter with Goliath, Saul and David pass each other —the latter on the way up, the former going down.

Our second query has to do with the motives of David. Namely, *Was David as loyal to Saul as the text implies? Or were there some well-founded reasons for Saul's suspicion of him?*

In all probability the truth lies somewhere between David's repeated assertions of loyalty and Saul's consuming distrust of him. If David were as loyal as he said, then one must wonder why he fashioned an insurgent army. There were other alternatives—self-exile, for example.

What is being suggested here is that Saul's doubts about David were not entirely groundless. In one sense David was a threat to Saul from the outset, his protests notwithstanding. Only a fool could miss it, and Saul was no fool!

David caught the public fancy. He was red-haired and youthful. He combined those two traits which endear men to women—a talent for warfare and a talent for song. To use an overworked term, David was charismatic. People found themselves attracted to him in spite of the potential dangers involved, as witness Jonathan's utter devotion to him. Jonathan, as heir to the throne, had the most to fear from David. Yet time after time he preserved David's life from the plottings of his father.

Perhaps Saul overestimated the threat which David held for himself and his dynasty, but he did not do so by much. The adulated young upstart from Bethlehem bore close watching by a first king of a very unstable monarchical system.

THE TRAGIC KING

The account of this man's life has been entitled "Saul: A Biblical Tragedy." The key descriptive word of the title was chosen with great care. One hears of this tragedy and that tragedy; but, in fact, the term possesses a fairly restricted meaning. One associates tragedy with an inexorable, crushing fate. In the great tragedies of literature, the factors which make for human catastrophe are present from the outset. The very first act sets before the audience the malign forces which drive the protagonist toward his doom.

Thus, one experiences no surprises in dramatic tragedy. The plot grinds irreversibly toward its predetermined end. Five minutes after we have become acquainted with a Willie Loman or a Hamlet or an Electra we know that, as the common saying goes, their fate is sealed. The fascination of tragic drama does not inhere in the play's conclusion, which is broadly understood from the outset. Rather, we are gripped by the *manner* in which the inescapable conclusion is reached.

It is in this sense that we can speak very precisely of the *tragedy* of Saul.

The forces which provoked his estrangement from Samuel, his consuming jealousy of David, his alienation from the members of his own family, his occasional fits of melancholia, all point toward a tragic end. The drums of fate are heard even as Saul is acknowledged ruler at Gilgal. Saul, then, is a tragic king. He is akin to Lear and Richard II and Macbeth and Oedipus.

We might pause briefly at this point in order to inquire into those aspects of emotional imbalance which played so great a part in Saul's doom. The first thing which must be said is that it is not at all surprising that Saul came to be crippled by severe neuroses. His tasks were enormous. Accordingly, his tasks were debilitating. There was the struggle to unify the tribes. There were the inevitable frictions which come about as the result of an untried political system. Besides all this there was the pressure of constant warfare.

At a more personal level, Saul suffered a number of telling misfortunes. The break with Samuel must have been an extremely traumatic experience. Saul was an intensely religious man. His dependence upon the prophet approached idolatry. The split amounted to a kind of excommunication, and it must have shattered the man.

David's insurgency added to his woes, not forgetting the fact that Saul's own children gave some measure of allegiance to their father's bitterest enemy.

Besides, there were the unspeakable and awesome cares and anxieties which every man harbors within himself.

Modern psychology would probably regard Saul as a manic
depressive with paranoid tendencies. From the limited knowledge we have of him, we can surmise that he must have
been more than ordinarily suspicious of other people. The
fear that others would harm him or usurp his place periodi-
cally threw him into a state of dissociative depression.

"An evil spirit from the LORD tormented him," is the way
I Samuel puts it—which, incidentally, provides a rather interesting and optimistic approach to mental illness, since
anything from the Lord is ultimately good, even an "evil
spirit." Anyway, from the depths of depression the court
musicians would try to raise him, using such grace notes
as were at their disposal. We are told that even David
engaged in this type of therapy.

Alternating with depression came unpredictable acts of
overt hostility, such as the attempt to thrust David through
with a javelin, or the demented slaughter of the priests of
Nob. Such behavior is typical in paranoia. When one can
no longer tolerate a threat, one attempts to eliminate it.
Persecution, imagined or real, is resolved by destroying the
persecutor.

GILBOA

As the last dolorous act of Saul's life begins, we find
that David has fled with his ragtag army through the Philistine lines, there to take up a career as something of a military adventurer. Could this have been an act of treachery
on David's part? Let the reader decide. All that can be
known for sure is that the author of the early source goes
to great lengths to assure us that David did not personally
participate as an ally of the Philistines in the last great battle
of Saul's life.

Gilboa was a mountain some fifty miles north of Saul's

capital in Gibeah. Its heights commanded the Plains of Es-
draelon, a strategic point of topography for the Philistines
because the plains were used as one of their primary trade
routes to the East. The site of this, Saul's last battle, indicates
the success with which he and his valiant men had driven
the Philistines from Israel. In a relatively short time the
tables had been completely turned. Saul had taken charge
of a defeated, subjugated nation and turned it into one of
the dominant forces in this part of the Near East.

Why was Saul fighting far north at Gilboa? There can
be only one answer. Saul meant to apply an economic strangle-
hold on his chief adversary. Had he won here, Saul would
doubtless be remembered as one of the most daring and
capable military commanders in history.

But he did not win at Gilboa. And it was not only because
the Philistines, desperate at the growing might of Israel,
had been able to gather an unusually large army. Saul had
faced overwhelming odds before, and without a qualm. Rather,
those drums of fate had begun to rise to a deafening cre-
scendo.

. . . when Saul saw the Philistine force, fear struck him to the
heart.

—I Samuel 28:5

Overwhelmed by anxieties, bereft of self-confidence, tor-
tured by nameless fears, weakened by lack of nourishment
—for he could not eat—Saul frantically began to search for
some sort of divine omen as to the outcome of the battle
close at hand. Failing to learn anything by the casting of
sacred lots (or dice), Saul began an immediate search for
some other form of supernatural communication.

Saul's disguised visit to the medium of Endor gives further
evidence of his shattered state of mind. After all, it was
he, Saul, who had devoutly fought the practice of necromancy

in Israel! Saul knew the divine prohibition against witchcraft! And he would have it no other way!

> Let no one be found among you who makes his son or daughter
> pass through fire, no augur or soothsayer or diviner or sorcerer,
> no one who casts spells or traffics with ghosts and spirits, and
> no necromancer. Those who do these things are abominable to
> the LORD.
>
> —Deuteronomy 18:10–12

Yet it is in the throes of black magic that we find Saul
in his last hours, violating one of the sternest dictates of
his religion.

One of the better interpretations of the seance in which
the spirit of the now-dead Samuel is summoned up has
been provided by Arthur Honegger in his oratorio *King
David*. This work provides an audial, not a visual, description. Coloring the words of the text are the dissonances of
twentieth-century music.

"Ommm . . . Omm," moans the medium as she goes
into her trance. In the background the instruments create
an atmosphere of gloom and mystery with a hint of the
satanic.

Suddenly the medium, having descended to other levels
of awareness, recognizes her muffled visitor as the archfoe
of witchcraft. She shrieks in terror, "You are Saul! Why
have you deceived me?"

We read in the twenty-eighth chapter of I Samuel that
Saul immediately informed the medium that there would
be no reprisal for her conducting the seance, then urged
her to continue. Reassured, the medium made contact with
Samuel's spirit.

> Samuel said to Saul, "Why have you disturbed me and brought
> me up?" Saul answered, "I am in great trouble; the Philistines

are pressing me and God has turned away; he no longer answers me through prophets or through dreams, and I have summoned you to tell me what I should do."

—I Samuel 28:15

Saul's attempt to curry some word of approval from his onetime friend and adviser is almost too pathetic to bear. The tragic king probably hoped that Samuel had come to understand things a bit better now that he had gone to abide within the shadows of Sheol.

But no. Once more Saul was reminded of his disobedience in the Amalekite incident. There followed the ghostly Samuel's dire prediction:

". . . the LORD will let your people Israel fall into the hands of the Philistines and, what is more, tomorrow you and your sons shall be with me."

—I Samuel 28:19

At these words, Saul fainted.

Whether the soldiers sensed their leader's distress that next day, or a rumor of the oracle of disaster had spread throughout the camp robbing men of their confidence, we cannot say. We only know that the Israelites were badly defeated at Gilboa. One by one Saul's sons were slain, including Jonathan, the brave young man upon whom Saul had set such high hopes.

Possibly Saul knew of Jonathan's death as the arrows of enemy archers began to find him. Possibly the pain of his wounds was compounded by the deeper pain of a father's grief over the death of his sons. Possibly he realized that there was no chance of making an escape. Possibly the like-lihood of capture was imminent. Possibly the picture of Samson may have flashed before him—Samson, the great rival of the Philistines who had ended his days "eyeless in

Gaza" and an object of scorn. Whatever it was that prompted
the ultimate act of despair, Saul, in the waning moments
of bitter defeat, took his own life—one of the few examples
of suicide to be found in the Scriptures.

> The Philistines hotly pursued Saul and his sons and killed the
> three sons, Jonathan, Abinadab and Malchishua. The battle went
> hard for Saul, for some archers came upon him and he was
> wounded in the belly by the archers. So he said to his armour-
> bearer, "Draw your sword and run me through, so that these
> uncircumcised brutes may not come and taunt me and make
> sport of me." But the armour-bearer refused, he dared not;
> whereupon Saul took his own sword and fell on it.
>
> —I Samuel 31:2–4

Learning of the disaster, David composed his great lament.
Of this incredibly moving poem, Old Testament scholar George
B. Caird has written, "On the merits of this one composition
David is entitled to a place among the writers of the world's
greatest lyric poetry."

Centuries have not diminished the feelings so freshly and
immediately exposed by this great dirge. Like the chorus of
a Greek drama, it sums up the emotions and provides a
catharsis for those who have encountered the tragedy of Saul.

O prince of Israel, laid low in death!
  How are the men of war fallen!

Tell it not in Gath,
proclaim it not in the streets of Ashkelon,
  lest the Philistine women rejoice,
  lest the daughters of the uncircumcised exult.

Hills of Gilboa, let no dew or rain fall on you,
  no showers on the uplands!
For there the shields of the warriors lie tarnished,
  and the shield of Saul, no longer bright with oil.

The bow of Jonathan never held back
from the breast of the foeman, from the blood of the slain;
the sword of Saul never returned
    empty to the scabbard.

Delightful and dearly loved were Saul and Jonathan;
    in life, in death, they were not parted.
They were swifter than eagles,
    stronger than lions.

Weep for Saul, O daughters of Israel!
    who clothed you in scarlet and rich embroideries,
    who spangled your dress with jewels of gold.

How are the men of war fallen, fallen on the field!
    O Jonathan, laid low in death!
I grieve for you, Jonathan my brother;
    dear and delightful you were to me;
your love for me was wonderful,
    surpassing the love of women.

Fallen, fallen are the men of war;
    and their armour left on the field.

                         —II Samuel 1:19–27

SAUL, SAUL . . .

A few words by way of a sequel.

Many, many years after these events, a Jewish couple living in the province of Cilicia on the southeastern shore of the Mediterranean would come to name one of their sons after the first king of Israel.

Did young Saul of Tarsus ever ponder the life of his namesake?

Undoubtedly he did. Everyone loves the sound of his own name. So when Saul would hear the stories of the first king of Israel, he no doubt became very attentive. It would not even be surprising if at one time the young Saul of Tarsus decided to model his life after the other Saul, though being careful to avoid Saul's "tragic flaw."

And what was that flaw?

According to the Scriptures it was his unwillingness to be totally obedient to the will of God as he knew it. God's will may have seemed to him arbitrary or senseless. It may even have been transmitted through arrogant and unworthy mediators. Nevertheless Saul shared with all of humanity the obligation to submit to that divine will.

And so young Saul of Tarsus may have pledged to follow God's beckonings however odd, however incredible. And, for him, how odd and incredible that will of God would turn out to be!

One other difference between the Sauls. The earlier of the two was one of Israel's most vigorous opponents of the Gentiles. The latter proved to be one of their most effective allies. One visited death upon them; the other, life. For Saul of Tarsus, later Paul the Apostle to the Gentiles, came to understand that God was greater than the divisions of men. It was this Saul who proclaimed that all were one in Christ—Jew and Gentile; yes, even Israelite and Philistine.

V THE FOOLISHNESS
OF SOLOMON

"Wise men in plenty are the world's salvation, and a prudent king is the sheet-anchor of his people. Learn what I have to teach you, therefore, and it will be for your good."

—Wisdom of Solomon

It might be useful to begin this character study with the reiteration that a childhood introduction to the Bible can be one of the most severely inhibiting factors in any adult appreciation of it. This happens when a person continues to mature in every other way, yet fails to exchange an infantile attitude about the Bible for an adult one.

There is nothing invariable about this condition. Yet it happens often enough to warrant a good deal of caution. There are any number of people on the fringes of the Church who have become religiously handicapped by their inability to shift gears from a Sunday school approach to the Bible to that of an adult.

The issue we have touched on here is called by Biblical scholars the problem of hermeneutics. The term is an imposing one, and should be used whenever one desires to make an impression. Nevertheless "hermeneutics" simply refers to the manner in which the content of the Bible is grasped and interpreted and utilized.

A wrong hermeneutics comes about when a person allows himself to become bound by those assumptions about the Bible which were drilled into him when he was a noisy little fellow down in that musty old Sunday school room in the church basement, the one with the out-of-tune piano. As the years have passed, he has continued to assume that the content of the Scriptures must be understood in precisely the same manner as that taught him at the age of seven. Or perhaps he supposes that the characters of a certain Biblical story must be regarded in precisely the same manner as that assigned to them back in the days when he wore his attendance badges like a hanging ladder upon his breast.

When, as a freshly ordained clergyman, I began developing programs of adult education in the church, I often found myself wondering why such a large percentage of members, even the very devout, found it so difficult to develop an interest in the study of the Bible. This book, after all, was supposed to be the source and standard of the Christian religion. One would expect churchmen to be eager to study its pages and discuss its doctrine. But this was not the case.

The reactions for this, I came to learn, were varied. There was, first of all, the fact that the study of the Bible was not easy. I found that many people expected to elicit all sorts of treasures from the Bible, but without any digging. When they found out that it did not work in quite this way, they quickly grew discouraged.

Still another and more subtle cause of disaffection with the Bible stemmed from the problem just alluded to. It was that many adults continued to cling to childish and dreadfully inadequate conceptions about the Bible. And not only this, but they felt that it verged on blasphemy to regard the Scriptures in any other way.

In time I came to see that the path to Biblical learning for many people began with a good deal of "unlearning."

The familiar, comfortable, credulous Sunday school attitudes had to be examined in an honest and critical manner; and, where wrong, abandoned.

This process was, for some, on the painful side. But I found that almost invariably there would follow some splendid insights into the message of the Bible, and a great deal of spiritual nurture besides.

It may seem a trifle unkind to suggest that the way in which dear old Miss Everlasting told us Bible stories could in any way prove a liability to adult Bible study. We cherish the memory of her oft-told accounts of Biblical heroes and villains. Nor do we forget the tidy morals which followed. Nor the illustrations she flashed before us. Dear heavens, the illustrations! Well-coifed, smooth-shaven people in immaculate bathrobes, lounging about splendidly pillared houses set within manicured gardens; and, in the middle distance, a marvelously deciduous forest without a single weed or dead branch.

We remember all this. And we revere it.

But still it is necessary to remember that childhood approaches to a book as vital as the Holy Bible are simply inadequate to adult needs.

Take, for example, the story of King Solomon. If I were to put down an accurate remembrance of my childhood understanding of this Old Testament figure, it would go something like this:

KING SOLOMON WAS A GREAT KING. HE WAS THE SON OF KING DAVID.

SHORTLY AFTER HE WAS CROWNED, GOD ASKED SOLOMON WHAT HE WOULD LIKE IN ORDER TO HELP HIM BE KING. EVERYONE EXPECTED SOLOMON TO SAY MONEY OR POWER OR SOMETHING OF THE SORT. BUT SOLOMON DID NOT ASK FOR THESE THINGS. INSTEAD HE ASKED FOR WISDOM. AND GOD WAS

SO PLEASED BY ALL THIS THAT HE PROMISED HIM MONEY AND
POWER ANYWAY.

AND WAS SOLOMON WISE AFTER THAT?

YOU BET YOUR LIFE HE WAS! ONE DAY TWO WOMEN CAME TO
HIM CLAIMING A SINGLE CHILD. SO SOLOMON MADE AS IF HE
WERE GOING TO CUT THE BABY IN TWO AND GIVE EACH WOMAN
HALF. BUT ONE OF THE WOMEN OBJECTED, SO SOLOMON KNEW
WHICH WAS THE REAL MOTHER.

BESIDES THIS STROKE, AS IT WERE, OF GENIUS, SOLOMON WAS
SO WISE THAT HE WROTE THE BOOK OF PROVERBS.

SOLOMON WAS NOT ONLY WISE. HE WAS RICH TOO! AND HE
HAD A GOOD MANY WIVES—BUT THAT WAS OKAY BECAUSE PEO-
PLE BELIEVED IN THAT THEN. BESIDES, HE BUILT THE TEMPLE,
WHICH WAS A VERY RELIGIOUS THING TO DO.

THE POINT OF IT ALL IS TO ASK GOD FOR THE RIGHT THING,
AND YOU MIGHT JUST GET A FEW BONUSES ON THE SIDE—LIKE
A LOT OF MONEY.

Now the trouble with this interpretation of the story of
King Solomon is that while it is somewhat accurate at certain
points, it is, in the main, wrong from start to finish. Indeed,
the over-all conception of Solomon here represents a colossal
failure to deal with the character and career of this king as
portrayed in the pages of the Bible.

A careful reading reveals that Solomon was not, in ac-
tuality, a very good king. The Scriptures tell us that while he
was very rich, he did not use his riches well. It does assert
that Solomon was wise, but it becomes readily apparent that
he was wise only in a very restricted sense of the word.
Indeed, in many ways Solomon was a very foolish man.

The point is that we can understand this only if we are
content to cast old preconceptions to the winds and investi-
gate Solomon as if we had never heard of him before.

By taking a fresh look at the career of Solomon as recorded

in the books of Kings and Chronicles, we cannot fail to reach certain conclusions. For example, the fact that his reign began as an idyll, but ended a nightmare. The fact that he found his country strong, unified, motivated; but left it bankrupt, divided, dispirited. The fact that his career began with a prayer for wisdom in the governing of his people—a prayer which God granted together with the promise of great wealth and honor. But among the repercussions of his death was the desperate plea of his subjects to Rehoboam his successor:

> "Your father laid a cruel yoke upon us; but if you will now lighten the cruel slavery he imposed on us and the heavy yoke he laid on us, we will serve you."
>
> —I Kings 12:4

It is curious that many Christians allow themselves to be so lenient with the character of Solomon. This is especially so when it is recalled that Solomon does not seem to have fared so well with his own people, either in his time or afterwards. One finds a strange silence about Solomon in the subsequent pages of Scripture. It is as though the less said about him the better, even though he was the ruler at the height of the united monarchy's prosperity, a time when the wealth and prestige of the people of God were at their crest.

Indeed, later generations seem to have found Solomon's father, King David, much more to their liking. They preferred David's hearfelt songs to Solomon's cleverness. They felt that there was something far more genuine in David's often eccentric practice of religion than in the polished, syncretistic ritual of Solomon's temple. And perhaps they came to understand that there was something far worse than the occasional and outrageous sins of David; namely, the jaded decadence of the court of Solomon.

Thus it is hardly surprising that when future generations looked back for an ideal kingdom upon which to base their future hopes, it was David's, not Solomon's, which would come to provide them with a model.

SOLOMON'S COUP

"He who brings trouble on his family inherits the wind."

—Proverbs

Solomon's reign of forty years (962–922 B.C.) did not, in fact, begin with his dream at Gibeon in which he prayed for wisdom. Rather it began with a far more conscious struggle for power.

In order to understand this, one must begin with the poignant picture of that dying lion, old King David, surrounded by court intriguers who were already warring over the succession.

There were two factions. The more prominent of them consisted of Adonijah who, as David's eldest surviving son, was the rightful heir to the throne; Joab, David's nephew and army commander; and Abiathar, David's court chaplain and intimate.

The other and shrewder faction included Bathsheba, the wife whom David obtained under such despicable circumstances and who was the mother of Solomon; Nathan the prophet; Zadok the priest; Benaiah the captain of the court guard; and Solomon himself.

Solomon's faction was clever not only for its ability to muster the support of the more influential courtiers, but also for its realization that the will of the stricken David was still potent enough to turn the tides of popular support.

The Solomon faction made its appeal to the dying David

in a manner which was both deft and timely. The members of the faction waited until the impatient Adonijah had proclaimed himself king. They then used this self-proclamation as a lever to win David's support, suggesting that Adonijah was so greedy for power that he could not properly await his father's death before grasping the crown. Such at least seems to have been the strategy of the Solomon faction. The details are not given in the Bible.

No sooner had Adonijah been traduced in the eyes of his father than Bathsheba arrived at David's deathbed with the reminder that he had once promised the throne to her son Solomon. Whether or not David had ever made such a promise is doubtful. Probably not, since such promises were so at odds with the prevailing ideas about heirdom.

David may well have been inclined to dismiss this information as little more than a mother's request for special favors for her child, when suddenly Nathan the prophet conveniently arrived with much the same message, reminding David that he had sworn to give the kingdom to Solomon.

This one-two combination, together with the innuendos about Adonijah, was sufficient to rouse the half-dead David. Immediately he proclaimed Solomon the rightful heir and ordered that he be anointed king forthwith.

We read that the shouts of acclamation which attended Solomon's investiture interrupted the festivities of the unsuspecting Adonijah faction.

> Then Adonijah's guests all rose in panic and scattered. Adonijah himself, in fear of Solomon, sprang up and went to the altar and caught hold of its horns.
>
> —I Kings 1:49–50

A typical bloodbath ensued, Solomon's pledge to the contrary notwithstanding. No sooner had King David died than

Solomon, under the flimsiest of pretexts, had his political
opponents put to the sword.

Solomon's hatchet man was Benaiah. There are few more
distasteful figures in the pages of the Bible. One by one
Benaiah dispatched the old faction: Adonijah—"Thereupon
King Solomon gave Benaiah son of Jehoiada his orders, and
he struck him down and he died." That doughty old warrior,
Joab—"So Benaiah son of Jehoiada went up to the altar and
struck Joab down and killed him. . . ." And Shimei, an old
family adversary—"The king then gave orders to Benaiah son
of Jehoiada, and he went out and struck Shimei down;
and he died."

How many more people were liquidated through the services of Benaiah we cannot know. The chronicler of these
events concludes this portion of the account of Solomon's
accession to the throne with these cryptic words:

Thus Solomon's royal power was securely established.

—I Kings 2:46

SOLOMON'S TEMPLE

"For the worship of idols . . . is the beginning, cause, and end
of every evil."

—Wisdom of Solomon

Before proceeding to some of the characteristics of Solomon's career as king, it might be instructive to give some
scrutiny to the construction of the temple for which he is
given so much unexamined credit.

We need not be concerned here with the details of the
temple's architecture, except to note that many people become surprised when they learn that this building was much

smaller than they might have imagined, being only the size of an ordinary classroom, which is to say about ninety feet long and thirty wide. Its diminutive size was compensated for in some measure by the surroundings and lavish ornamentation. Still one is left with the suspicion that the temple seems to have been designed more for use as a royal chapel than as a "house of prayer for all people."

Of more profound significance is the fact that the construction of the temple tended to restrict the supposed presence of Jahweh to a single, fixed place. This centralization of religion marked a definite transition in the development of the religion of Israel, and not an altogether good one at that.

In order to understand this, we must recall that the Israelites gained one of their greatest insights into the nature of God because of their wanderings. When they lived as nomads in the wilderness, they came to realize that God too was always on the move. Jahweh went where the people went. His dwelling place was in the midst of the congregation, wherever that congregation happened to be. Hence the tabernacle, the movable tent of worship, which always accompanied the Israelites during their wanderings.

Israel's concept of Jahweh's omnipresence always posed a sharp contrast to the shrine mentality of the pagan religions about her; which is to say, the notion that the gods were restricted to certain fixed sacred places.

Scholars tend to believe that the building of the temple indicated the presence of some rather serious inroads of Canaanitic religion into the worship of Israel. They point out, for instance, that the design of the temple was based on Syrian prototypes, or that its accouterments were, in certain cases, identical with those used in Baal-Ashtoreth fertility ceremonial, a fact which is not at all surprising when it is remembered that the chief designer, Hiram, was in all probability a Phoenician. One commentator notes that

the pillars which stood at the entrance to the temple were
called "the sides of the north" in other cults, and that such
pillars were to be found at the entrances to temples at Tyre,
Shechem, Byblos, Hierapolis, Paphos, Sardis, Khorsbad and
elsewhere in the Near and Middle East. In addition, fertility symbols dominated much of the temple decor—palm,
pomegranates, bulls, to name a few.

Besides the Canaanitic motif, there is the distinct possibility that the temple was actually used for pagan rites
which were conducted for the benefit of Solomon's foreign
wives, of which more later.

SOLOMON'S SLAVES

"He who oppresses the poor insults his Maker."

—Proverbs

Without doubt the most shocking aspect of the temple's
construction is the fact that it was built through means of
forced labor. One account of Solomon's construction program,
that of II Chronicles, attempts to mitigate the offense by
claiming that only foreigners were impressed into service.
The other and more contemporary account found in I Kings,
however, acknowledges that a levy of thirty thousand Israelites were conscripted into the building program.

To what extent the statistics of forced labor recorded in
these two books are accurate is hard to tell. But even if
only a small number of aliens were forced to work in the
quarries, it seems, given Israel's solemn remembrance of slavery in Egypt and the religious proscriptions against the
practice which ensued, that even a few slaves were too
many.

The unfortunate aftermath of this was that the custom of
slavery became entrenched in Israel's life during the reign

of Solomon. It was not extirpated until the defeat of Israel and Judah some centuries later.

We must not, of course, judge Solomon purely from the perspective of our own age with its enlightened attitudes regarding human rights. Yet it must be recognized that even according to his own lights, Solomon was running counter to some of the most hallowed traditions of his ancestors when he instituted the corvée for the furtherance of his construction projects.

In passing, it is instructive to note that the building of cathedrals and churches and temples and shrines have always brought out the best and the worst in men. They have elicited great quantities of self-sacrifice. They have provided evidence of a deep desire to aspire to a truer worship of God. But there has always come an accompanying temptation to become so concerned with the glories of worship that the concerns of men have become forgotten.

Is it not one of the terrible ironies of human history that men have erected their tributes to God on the bruised and broken backs of their wretched fellow humans? In our own day we have become more sophisticated. We no longer enslave people to build our churches. But we still go on spending vast percentages of tithed money on church construction and, more particularly, expensive paper-shuffling church bureaucracies, while much of the world suffers from physical and spiritual destitution.

Solomon's temple provides a dramatic reminder of the impossibility of separating means and ends—either in his day or ours. The chief end of man may be to glorify God and enjoy him forever, but we must not attempt to reach this end by inhuman means, such as the practice of slavery. For means shape ends. Means determine ends. Means have a way of *becoming* ends. As Christ noted, there is absolutely no way of getting good fruit (ends) from bad trees (means).

Another way of looking at the problem might be to say that if Solomon had less of an edifice mentality, and more of a ministry mentality, the temple would never have been built.

SOLOMON'S WEALTH

"He who trusts in riches will wither."

—Proverbs

"Better a pittance honestly earned than great gains ill gotten."
—Proverbs

That Solomon was a man of great wealth cannot be doubted. That he was an extravagant spender likewise cannot be doubted.

Solomon did not happen to be the type to accumulate wealth. The money merely poured through his hands. Solomon, to be blunt about it, was a spendthrift. On at least one occasion his prodigalities brought the nation to the verge of bankruptcy. Only by ceding certain cities in the northern part of Israel to a neighboring king was he able to avert the financial crisis.

As noted, a great part of Solomon's wealth went toward his various construction projects. Solomon was an inveterate builder. When he built, he did so on a grand scale. The palace complex, the temple, the immense fortifications built at strategic locations throughout Israel and Judah, the seaports and landports, the mining centers, the metal refineries, the special cities, the stables and granaries—all of these seem to have been erected impulsively and without regard to cost.

A large portion of the king's resources went toward the maintenance of his court. Solomon's reign reached a peak of ostentation and luxury unmatched in Israel's history, either before or after. The contrast between Solomon's style of living and the much more simple tastes of his father, not to mention the positively rustic habits of King Saul, doubtless caused a great deal of headshaking among the older of his overtaxed subjects. A careful reading of the various accounts of his reign indicates the presence of not only a certain pride in Solomon's affluence, but a detectable uneasiness as well. The opulent adornments and gorgeous appointments are listed: the ivory throne, the golden utensils, the cedar paneling, the precious stones, the inexhaustible silver, the continual arrival of tribute shipments—textiles and precious metals, ivory, myrrh and spices, horses, peacocks and apes. But little significance is attached to the inventory.

How was it that Solomon was so wealthy? What were the forces which channeled the riches of the Levant to his court?

Solomon's wealth seems to have been the result of three separate, yet dovetailed factors.

First there was the great organizational ability of the man. Shortly after taking the throne, Solomon organized Israel and Judah into twelve districts, each of which was governed by a prefect. The primary duty of these prefects, it seems, was to raise tax revenues. Each district, for example, was obliged to support the palace expenses for a month of each year—quite an expense, considering the size of Solomon's court!

The ruthless efficiency with which Solomon's taxes were collected is indicated by the solidarity which backed the northern revolt shortly after Solomon's death. The grievances were widespread. Everyone had felt the weight of Solomon's internal revenue system. Jeroboam, the political rebel, had little difficulty in enlisting popular support.

Another reason for Solomon's wealth must be assigned to his unusually acute business sense. Solomon was a great capitalist. He understood from the start the importance of

L.I.F.E. College Library
1100 Glendale Blvd.
Los Angeles, Calif. 90026

Israel's strategic location in the economy of the Middle East, and he made good use of it.

During Solomon's reign a series of trading routes, both land and sea, were established. Under the king's stimulation, goods were kept flowing from Spain in the west to the Euphrates in the east; from the coast of East Africa to the south, to the shores of the northern Mediterranean.

Solomon's indigenous business interests centered on mining and smelting. He has been called "the king of copper." He also profited greatly by the collection of tolls from the caravans which plied the roads running from Mesopotamia to Egypt.

Trading, above all else, was Solomon's forte. Interestingly, one of the primary media of Solomon's trading enterprises seems to have been horses. One might say that Solomon was basically a horse trader, and a very good one at that. There is some indication that he held a virtual monopoly on the distribution of horses and chariots in the Levant. The massive complex of stables uncovered at Megiddo tends to support the theory. Is it too far-fetched to suggest that Solomon may have been a devotee of horse racing? Not entirely. The Scriptures do not say so, but it seems quite in keeping with the other information we have of him.

Of greatest importance for the affluence of King Solomon was the relative quiescence of the great powers above and below Israel. During his time there was little danger from either Egypt or Mesopotamia. The importance of this fact cannot be overstressed, especially when it is recalled that the history of Israel seems largely an account of being over-run by armies from either one side or the other.

Beyond the fact of Solomon's wealth and the reasons for it lies the issue of how it was used. Hensley Henson once wrote, "The use to which we put our possessions is, perhaps, as good a test of our religion as we can find." According to such a test as this, Solomon failed miserably. He achieved great wealth; but, from all evidences, he spent it neither wisely nor well. His was a spendthrift regime. The money came in great quantities, but there is little indication that it was ever used for the general weal of the people. Indeed, the major part of it was evidently used for the fancies and pleasures of Solomon himself.

A pertinent observation for the times relates to the fact that a great deal of Solomon's money went toward the construction of lavish and eventually useless fortifications. The country came to be defeated not through outside forces. Rather it fell apart from within, the victim of the malaise which comes of flagrant spending, unendurable taxation and the continual threat of national insolvency. Surely the best defense spending has never been that spent on weapons and fortifications, either then or now.

It may sound curious to say so, but the problem with Solomon's wealth was its cost. Eventually the price of it proved too great.

Consider the bill which Solomon left the nation after his death:

Item: An overtaxed people with nothing to show for their returns but a mammoth defense establishment of dubious worth and a great deal of high living in the capital.

Item: The bitter enmity of the tribes which surrounded Israel, tribes whose fathers and sons had been impressed into the forced labor battalions needed for Solomon's building program.

Item: The increasing envy of the nations around Israel, who not only cast covetous eyes on the splendor of Jerusalem, but may have come to understand that the only way to prevent economic gouging along the trade routes was to keep Israel weak and balkanized.

"And the king made silver as common in Jerusalem as stone," they wrote of him. But it did not remain that way

long after his death. The collectors made their demands. The
bill was paid. And the united monarchy, fashioned la-
boriously by Saul and David, was through.

SOLOMON'S WIVES

"Rejoice in the wife of your youth."

—Proverbs

"Enjoy life with the wife whom you love."

—Ecclesiastes

The two passages quoted above are taken from a context
in which monogamous marriage is idealized. It is hard to
believe that these words could have been written by Solomon. Here was a man, we are told, who had seven hundred wives and three hundred concubines.

Allowing for a certain amount of exaggeration on the part
of the authors, we are still left, in Solomon's case, with a
royal household which makes that of the King of Siam seem
like little more than tea for two.

Consider the ratio! One thousand to one! Or try to imagine
the atmosphere which must have pervaded the palace! Contemplate, if you can, all those women and their offspring
with nothing to do all day but trade rumors for gossip, and
gossip for intrigue, and intrigue for plots, and plots for coun-
terplots! Perhaps, on second thought, Solomon may have
come to have a very high regard indeed for monogamous
marriage!

No doubt many of Solomon's wives were the result of
political alliances. Cementing relationships with neighboring
rulers by marrying royal daughters remained a common state
policy until very recently. The special place accorded Pharaoh's daughter—she was given her own palace—indicates

that very important diplomatic relations were achieved with the ruler of Egypt.

Still, the dimensions of Solomon's harem goes beyond all precedent, and suggest a sensuality and luxury which ran counter to the traditions of the Hebrew people. It must be recalled that the polygamy practiced by the forebears of Solomon was largely an insurance that every woman have a husband and children. On certain occasions this would mean that a woman would have to share her husband with one or two other women, a situation which was common during times of military action when the male population would be decimated.

But the ideal of conjugal love and fidelity between a single man and a single woman has very ancient roots in the Judeo-Christian tradition. The creation narrative itself sets the limits. And if there were occasional instances of multiple wives, there was never any precedent for the monstrosity which was Solomon's harem.

There was one particularly grave aspect to the multiplicity of Solomon's wives. The author of I Kings put it this way:

King Solomon was a lover of women, and besides Pharaoh's daughter he married many foreign women, Moabite, Ammonite, Edomite, Sidonian, and Hittite, from the nations with whom the LORD had forbidden the Israelites to intermarry, "because," he said, "they will entice you to serve their gods." But Solomon was devoted to them and loved them dearly. He had seven hundred wives, who were princesses, and three hundred concubines, and they turned his heart from the truth. When he grew old, his wives turned his heart to follow other gods, and he did not remain wholly loyal to the LORD his God as his father David had been. He followed Ashtoreth, goddess of the Sidonians, and Milcom, the loathsome god of the Ammonites. Thus Solomon did what was wrong in the eyes of the LORD, and was not loyal to the LORD like his father David. He built a hill-shrine for Kemosh, the loathsome

god of Moab, on the height to the east of Jerusalem, and for
Molech, the loathsome god of the Ammonites. Thus he did for
the gods to which all his foreign wives burnt offerings and made
sacrifices.

—I Kings 11:1–8

SOLOMON'S WISDOM

"Dead flies make the perfumer's sweet ointment turn rancid
and ferment; so can a little folly make wisdom lose its worth."
—Ecclesiastes

Again and again in the pages of the Bible we are reminded that Solomon was a very wise man. One of the most
fetching stories of a king's good intentions at the beginning
of his reign is that of Solomon's prayer for wisdom. There
follows the story of how a shrewd maneuver enabled Solomon to distinguish between genuine mother love and the
envy and bitterness of a bereaved woman.

That story, incidentally, serves another purpose. It suggests that at the beginning of his rule, there was no problem
too small, no segment of society too mean for the attention
of the young king. Whether or not Solomon kept up this
interest in the problems of all his people throughout the
forty years of his reign is exceedingly doubtful.

The legacy of Solomon's wisdom is reputed to be contained in one apocryphal and three canonical books traditionally attributed to him: Proverbs, Ecclesiastes, Song of Solomon, and the Wisdom of Solomon. Further he is credited with
the authorship of three thousand proverbs and one thousand
and five songs.

One of the more fascinating indications of Solomon's wisdom has to do with the visit of the fabled Queen of Sheba.
That this woman must have been exceptional in every way

is witnessed to by the fact that she was one of the few female rulers of her time. Her country was located in south-western Arabia, and straddled some of the more important trade routes of that day, a fact which leads some commentators to believe that the primary purpose of her visit was business.

In all probability, the Queen of Sheba had also heard of Solomon's quick mind. Since she herself came from a culture in which the promulgation of proverbs and riddles was something of a national pastime, she put Solomon to the test. Solomon's display of mental gymnastics convinced her.

> "The report which I heard in my own country about you and your wisdom was true, but I did not believe it until I came and saw for myself. Indeed I was not told half of it; your wisdom and your prosperity go far beyond the report I had of them."
>
> —I Kings 10:6–7

Solomon seems to have possessed a curious turn of mind. It is interesting to read that this man, who lived nearly three thousand years ago, was apparently a student of the natural sciences. I Kings describes him as an amateur botanist and zoologist.

> He discoursed of trees, from the cedar of Lebanon down to the marjoram that grows out of the wall, of beasts and birds, of reptiles and fishes.
>
> —I Kings 4:33

Yet, from what we have discovered about the totality of his personality, it must be acknowledged that Solomon was wise only in a very restricted sense of that word. That he possessed wit and shrewdness cannot be argued. That he was bright and clever must be admitted by all. He was, unquestionably, a master of repartee. His proverbs show his love for the finely turned phrase. We can assume that he was fond of puns and double-entendre and all of the other forms of humor which one associates with education plus a native intelligence.

The question is, however, are such capacities and talents to be confused with true wisdom? Do cleverness and sagacity amount to the same thing? Is the man who is witty also necessarily wise? Can one say that a person who is quick on the verbal draw, who has a bon mot for every occasion, is by the same token profound? Is he not frequently quite the opposite?

Perhaps we can best answer our questions by asking once more what true wisdom, in fact, is. We shall not go to the dictionary for our definition, but rather remind ourselves of those people in history whose depth and vision have given mankind an understanding of what genuine wisdom ought to be.

The first thing with which we are struck when recalling the wise men of history is that they always seemed to combine insight with action. Men like Socrates, Gautama Buddha, Sir Thomas More and Abraham Lincoln—to employ a very diverse selection—not only had the ability to see deeply into the nature of things, but also had the desire and the courage to act accordingly.

Wisdom, it would seem, demands not only mental agility, but strong character as well. And it is precisely here that Solomon failed. Solomon's intelligence never seemed to have motivated him to any particular righteousness or cause or goal.

Because of this, Solomon must be assigned to a particular species of men who have always been regarded as clever, but never as particularly wise. Solomon belongs in the company of the proverb-makers of history, the prudent uncommitted—men like La Rochefoucauld and Lord Chesterfield and Benjamin Franklin: men who were clever, but hardly wise. Indeed on occasion each of them showed themselves to be utter fools.

Dare we flout the old traditions? Dare we say that Solomon was a fool?

Let us answer with a conjecture. According to the four Gospels, Jesus mentions Solomon by name only a very few times. Most will remember that in his Sermon on the Mount, Jesus noted that despite his costly adornment, Solomon was no match for the common wild lily.

One cannot help wonder, however, if Jesus may not have had Solomon in mind when he told one of his most trenchant stories—the story of a man who became so absorbed by his affluence that he found no time for other and more important considerations in life.

Read carefully this parable of the Rich Fool, and judge for yourself!

"There was a rich man whose land yielded heavy crops. He debated with himself: 'What am I to do? I have not the space to store my produce. This is what I will do,' said he: 'I will pull down my storehouses and build them bigger. I will collect in them all my corn and other goods, and then say to myself, "Man, you have plenty of good things laid by, enough for many years: take life easy, eat, drink, and enjoy yourself."' But God said to him, 'You fool, this very night you must surrender your life; you have made your money— who will get it now?' That is how it is with the man who amasses wealth for himself and remains a pauper in the sight of God."

—St. Luke 12:17–21

VI JEZEBEL:
A STUDY IN FANATICISM

And the LORD said to him,
  Call him Jezreel; for in a little while I will punish the line
  of Jehu for the blood shed in Jezreel and put an end to
  the kingdom of Israel.

—Hosea

JERUSALEM (Special Dispatch)—Rumors of the death of
Queen Mother Jezebel of the Northern Kingdom of Israel
continue to flow into this capital city of Jerusalem.

The reports remain unconfirmed. Regular communications
with the city of Jezreel, where the alleged event took place,
have been broken since the outbreak of the rebellion led by
General Jehu and his junta.

Observers here regard Queen Jezebel as one of the most
influential political forces in Israel's old regime. Consequently,
it is felt that should the revolution succeed, General Jehu will
not be inclined to spare her life.

If current rumors prove accurate, then the name of Jezebel
must be added to the growing list of victims in the present
insurgency. Her death will have closely followed that of her
son, King Jehoram.

Palace authorities in Queen Jezebel's home city of Tyre,
Phoenicia, are reportedly attempting to secure her safekeeping.
A strongly worded communique has been forwarded by the

government of Phoenicia to General Jehu's headquarters north of Jezreel within the past thirty-six hours. As yet no reply has been received.

A palace spokesman informed the press this morning that if Queen Jezebel has already fallen victim to the alleged atrocities of the army of General Jehu, it is yet hoped that her remains will be treated with the respect and dignity due a member of the Phoenician royal house.

Locally, Queen Athaliah of Judah has refused to make any comment on the rumored death of her mother. Sources close . . .

JERUSALEM (Update)—Eyewitness reports of the death of Queen Jezebel have been received here in Jerusalem within the hour. According to unimpeachable sources, the Queen was hurled from a palace window and trampled to death by charioteers under the personal command of General Jehu.

It is reported here that Queen Athaliah has gone into seclusion.

JERUSALEM (Obit)—Jezebel, wife of the late King Ahab of Israel, was not a native Israelite. A member of the ruling Phoenician dynasty, she was reared by her father, King Ethbaal, in the environs of the city of Tyre on the Mediterranean coast.

The queen's marriage to King Ahab took place just over thirty years ago. It was widely regarded as the marriage of the century, providing as it did the basis for a political alliance between Israel and Phoenicia.

According to most observers, the marriage turned out very satisfactorily. The royal pair had a number of children, some of whom have since become rulers in their own right.

Queen Jezebel was known as a person of pronounced religious opinions. A lifelong acquaintance said recently, "She was a true daughter to her father. She kept the religion of her childhood to the end." What was referred to is the fact that Jezebel's father, King Ethbaal, also served as a priest in the official Baal religion of Tyre.

Upon taking up residence in Israel, Queen Jezebel brought
with her many religious artifacts and clergy to minister to
her spiritual needs. As the years passed, she came to be known
as a most persuasive proponent of the religion of Baal. Many
people were converted to her religion during her years in
Israel.

Queen Jezebel's proseltyzing activities, however, earned her
many enemies. Among the most vocal of these was Elijah,
the Jahweh prophet from Tishbe.

Persons associated with the royal family indicate that
Jezebel's late husband, King Ahab, was deeply influenced by
her religious fervor, especially toward the end of his life. There
were persistent reports that he was considering a formal conversion to the religion of Baal.

Despite her Phoenician background, Queen Jezebel came to
look upon Israel as her home. After her husband's death on
the battlefield of Ramoth-Gilead, Jezebel elected to remain in
Israel with her sons.

Of her sons, Ahaziah, the eldest, succeeded his father to
the throne. His reign was a very short one. Shortly after his
succession, Ahaziah was killed in an accidental fall.

Queen Jezebel's next eldest son, Jehoram, assumed the crown
upon the death of his brother. Jehoram has since become a
victim of the current revolution . . .

The foregoing contrived wire service reports describe the
end of the Omri dynasty in Israel almost one thousand years
before the time of Christ. In particular they tell of the violent
ending of a queen's life.

Behind the impersonal, precise, journalistic prose, one
can sense the stark horror of it all: an ignoble death for the
queen herself, a decimation of her family, her adopted
country thrown into a state of confusion and revolt.

The pity of it is that it did not have to end that way.
The beginning was far different. The beginning was splendid
and full of hope. What intervened is the subject of our story.

INTO THE IVORY PALACES

Things must have looked promising for Israel when the young prince Ahab brought home his bride Jezebel, a princess from the nearby city of Tyre. The time was nearly twenty-eight hundred years ago, some nine hundred years before the birth of Christ.

Of the two kingdoms, Israel and Judah, which had emerged from the political schism following King Solomon's death, Israel, the northern kingdom, was clearly superior.

Israelites must have felt fairly confident about their future. They were militarily secure. Judah was no problem. Moab had been disarmed. Phoenicia was now an ally. The Syrians were restive, but checked. And of the succession of capital cities, Samaria, the most recent, was the safest of the lot.

Shortly after his marriage, Ahab succeeded his father, King Omri, to the throne. For the occasion an anonymous poet penned a tribute to the royal couple. Quite possibly his composition was said or sung at the enthronement ceremony. In time this poem found its way into the book of Psalms.

Many Christians of a conservative stripe might be a trifle shocked to learn that the psalm from which the central phrase for the gospel hymn "Out of the Ivory Palaces" was taken originated as a festive tribute to Ahab and Jezebel. But there it is!

My heart is stirred by a noble theme,
in a king's honour I utter the song I have made,
   and my tongue runs like the pen of an expert scribe.

   You surpass all mankind in beauty,
   your lips are moulded in grace,
so you are blessed by God for ever.
With your sword ready at your side, warrior king,

ride on to execute true sentence and just judgement.
Your right hand shall show you a scene of terror:
your sharp arrows flying, nations beneath your feet,
    the courage of the king's foes melting away!

Your throne is like God's throne, eternal,
    your royal sceptre a sceptre of righteousness.
You have loved right and hated wrong;
so God, your God, has anointed you
    above your fellows with oil, the token of joy.
Your robes are all fragrant with myrrh and powder of aloes,
    and the music of strings greets you
    from a palace panelled with ivory.
A princess takes her place among the noblest of your women,
    a royal lady at your side in gold of Ophir.

Listen, my daughter, hear my words
    and consider them:
forget your own people and your father's house;
and, when the king desires your beauty,
    remember that he is your lord.
Do him obeisance, daughter of Tyre,
and the richest in the land will court you with gifts.

    In the palace honour awaits her;
    she is a king's daughter,
    arrayed in cloth-of-gold richly embroidered.
Virgins shall follow her into the presence of the king;
    her companions shall be brought to her,
escorted with the noise of revels and rejoicing
    as they enter the king's palace.

    You shall have sons, O king, in place of your forefathers and will
    make them rulers over all the land.
I will declare your fame to all generations;
therefore the nations will praise you for ever and ever.

                                                    —Psalm 45

    Quite possibly some of the older people shook their heads
over the new queen. Interreligious marriages were, after all,

forbidden by the sacred law. And besides, the new queen showed no intention whatever of changing to the religion of Israel. Quite the contrary. Jezebel was not only a pagan, she was a steadfast pagan! A devout pagan! A pious pagan! She had even brought to Israel her own retinue of clergy. Over eight hundred of them! Whatever could one lone woman want with eight hundred religious functionaries? And, if that were not bad enough, there were rumors that Ahab had agreed to erect a temple to her god Baal at public expense!

If the young people of that day were anything like our own, we can surmise that they were far more open in the matter. They were, quite likely, interested in comparative religion, as young people have always tended to be. Some probably declared that all religions were good and made a plea for tolerance. Others maintained darkly that all religions were bad. And still others held that everything was relative. Then there were some who discovered that this new religion of Jezebel made for a pretty swinging scene.

There was ample reason for them to think so. The religion of Baal was essentially a nature religion. It spiritualized the mystery of fertility and reproduction. At its best it was a mild, bucolic pantheism. But at its worst it degenerated into the sexual debauchery of cult prostitution and ritual orgy.

Still it was relevant, no doubt of that! That was the problem with Baalism! Those who like their religion uncritically relevant would have approved of Baalism. Baalism met the religious needs of the ever increasing numbers of farmers in Israel. It held far more immediate meaning for the planting and harvesting of crops than that stern old ethical religion of Jahweh. The notion that one could actually influence the growth of his crops by sympathetic sexual activities was as pleasurable as it was plausible in those days when magic had a deep hold on the popular mentality.

Jahwism, on the other hand, with its emphasis on guidance and protection and dependence and no-nonsense morality seemed more suited to nomads than villagers, to herdsmen than farmers. And the truth of it is that Israel was now more agricultural than pastoral.

Yet, despite the simmering religious situation, the future of Israel seemed bright.

A SURFEIT OF RELIGION

Still it can be argued that when the spirit of religious fanaticism is abroad, the future can never be bright.

When the famous Brighton preacher, F. W. Robertson, advised his congregation to avoid joining "those fierce associations which think only of uprooting error," he was giving some very sound advice. Bigotry is, quite simply, dangerous. Bigotry provides the quickest, most efficient route to deeds of cruelty and injustice and bloodshed.

The fires of the Inquisition, the massacre on the day of that martyred apostle St. Bartholomew, the witch hunts at Salem, the ovens of Dachau—all had their beginnings in that attitude of ideological arrogance we call fanaticism. Nor should any Christian ever forget that the execution of Jesus Christ began as a conspiracy against him by a few religious fanatics.

So, when Ahab retired to his ivory-paneled palace with his queen after the enthronement ceremonies, his subjects looked forward to a long period of peace and progress. What the Israelites did *not* know on that festive day was that an excess of religiosity was about to undo them.

From where did this epidemic of fanaticism come?

Leaving to one side the fact that the germs of fanaticism lurk in every human breast, we are obliged, in the case at hand, to lay the major share of the blame with Queen Jezebel, more particularly her evident desire to convert Israel to her own religion.

That this was Jezebel's intention can hardly be argued. That she had the necessary initiative and intelligence to bring about her intentions is also quite certain. She was an impressive woman, this Jezebel. The Bible's portrait of her is hardly sympathetic. She is depicted as being one of the greatest threats to the faith of Israel since the time of the exodus. A genuine heresiarch!

Yet the Biblical writers do not obscure the fact that she was a remarkable woman. A foreigner in a xenophobic nation, a woman in a patriarchal society, still she was able to wield a mighty influence. Her humorlessness, her determination, her single-mindedness, her courage (and religious zealots ordinarily possess enormous reservoirs of sheer animal courage), all come through.

There is no speculation in the Scriptures as to why Jezebel was so intent on converting Israel to the worship of Baal. We wonder. Was it a shrewd maneuver on her part to unite Phoenicia and Israel through a common religion? Or was it, more simply, unadulterated fanaticism? We do not know. But we are bound to suspect the latter.

Whichever, the shrewd young queen cannot have failed to discern a shift in religious winds in Israel. Jahwism, she concluded, was on the skids. It had been all right as a religion so long as the Israelites had wandered around in the wilderness. But now that they had developed a viable political system, now that they had a king and economic stability and foreign relations, something more suitable was needed.

Jezebel, apparently, felt that she had the answer. Through the large number of religious functionaries she had brought with her from Phoenicia (missionaries, in a sense), through lavish public ceremonies, through the open sympathy of Ahab, and through the introduction of certain syncretistic practices, Jezebel set about her self-appointed task of converting Israel to the religion of Baal.

We are bound to infer, however, that Jezebel did not proceed with her mission of converting Israel in that spirit of open-mindedness and fair play which characterizes religious debate at its best and most creative. No one who reads the book of II Kings can avoid the unmistakable indications of religious bigotry in the character of Jezebel. One sees in her a compulsiveness, a rigidity, a dogmatism, an attitude of religious superiority which is all too familiar. Jezebel, in short, seems to have been an outright fanatic.

There is nothing either new or old about such fanaticism as hers. It is as old as man, as new as this morning's paper. Fanaticism remains one of the most virulent diseases of the spirit of man. It is religion in its most cancerous form.

How can one detect this disease? There are many symptoms, chiefly the following three:

1. *Religious certitude.* Even the most devout believer is obliged to acknowledge that of all branches of human knowledge, that which has to do with religious affirmation is based on the flimsiest evidence of all. Faith, as opposed to observation, or demonstration, or any other form of empirical validation, is the basis upon which one makes religious assertions. Consequently, such assertions must be regarded as being both tentative and highly subjective.

Despite this, the fanatic endows his religious speculations with absolute certitude, indeed with an iron positiveness which he would be ashamed to apply to any other area of human experience. A fanatic would never vent his opinions on the relative merits of various automobiles or gasolines or the best way to Toledo with the inflexible convictions he attaches to his theological system.

The fanatic is not only completely certain about the more trivial aspects of his beliefs. You will also find him just as certain about such mind-boggling cosmic eventualities as the timetables of Judgment Day, and he will gladly relate the details to anyone who will listen.

In all of this one can detect certain obsessive characteristics. The fanatic is consumed by the object of his fanaticism. All other facets of life which might provide him with concern or amusement—sports, music, public affairs, literature, social concerns, travel and so forth—are sacrificed to the cause in which he has immersed himself. A fanatic is never a well-rounded person. Nor is he apt to be a loving person. All of his energies are channeled in one direction only.

2. *Intolerance.* A second trait found in all fanatics is their intolerance. One cannot fail to recognize the manifest paranoia in fanaticism. The fanatic views religious opinions differing from his own as not merely erroneous. He sees them as a *threat!* They are malicious and perverse. Most fanatics, if they had the power, would put down all opposing doctrines with the sword, using for justification the old, blood-soaked theory that error has no rights.

Moreover, the fanatic tends to magnify the power of his religious opponents. His adversaries are always on the verge of overwhelming him. Consequently he is a pessimist. The world, he believes, gets worse and worse. He reads of catastrophes and wars with a certain grim satisfaction, for they seem to authenticate his bleak outlook. The fanatic lives on the fringes of Armageddon. He will tell you that the enemies of God (for which read *his* enemies, real or imagined) are about to take over.

Accompanying the fanatic's pessimism is an entrenched opposition to anything new. For the fanatic there is never any new truth, just as Jezebel seemed shut to the possibility of any new religious insight when she arrived in Israel. The fanatic regards the new as dangerous, diabolical. The old ways are the best ways, the true ways, and all deviation is regarded as being little more than further indication that the world is going to hell in a handcart.

3. *Proselytizing.* Finally, the fanatic is a compulsive proselytizer. He sees his mission in life as converting people, as bringing them to believe exactly as he does. In so doing, however, he rarely makes it easy for someone to accept his beliefs. You will ordinarily find him adding a few theological gimcracks to his system which are so patently absurd that no one in his right mind could possibly accept them. But this, he tells you, is the real test of faith.

By regarding fanaticism as the severe character disorder which it undoubtedly is, one is driven to the realization that the fanatic is *obliged* to proselytize! He is under compulsion to make converts! His psychological stability depends on it!

Why? Simply because of the reassurance derived thereby.

Anyone's ego gets a little boost when he is able to change the opinion of another through his powers of persuasion. But when a person is constantly unsure of himself, as fanatics tend to be underneath their bravado, when his ego strengths are barely sufficient to carry him along, such bolstering becomes a necessity. It assures a person that he *is* right, after all, and that his opinions *do* count for something, and that he *can* influence the attitudes of others. Such reassurance is a narcotic for the pathologically insecure people who swell the ranks of religious fanaticism.

Jezebel, from all indications, was in the mold. The evidence of a closed mind, of a narrowness of outlook saturates the oral tradition which underlies the Old Testament account of her career. She is remembered as a despiser of the religion of Jahweh. Her obsessive efforts to convert Israel to Baalism indicates that, like all fanatics, Jezebel was driven by certain demons of the mind.

But there was one not-so-typical thing about Jezebel. To wit, her power. Jezebel was a queen. And she was not a paper queen, not by a long shot. She was one of the few women in Israel's history to have become a genuine political force in her own right.

Power and fanaticism! These two factors in combination made of Jezebel a very dangerous woman.

THE CONTEST ON MOUNT CARMEL

Jezebel very nearly succeeded in her ambitions. When one of her harried religious opponents notified Jahweh that he was the only one of his believers left in Israel, he assumed that he was providing the Lord with nothing less than the facts.

To be sure, Jahweh answered him with the assurance that there were still "seven thousand in Israel . . . who have not bent the knee to Baal." But one can ask if even this answer was all that consoling. We do not know the population of Israel in those days, but it seems safe to suppose that seven thousand represented a distinct minority.

If it had not been for this particular opponent, Jezebel might have completely converted Israel to Baalism. Yet this man, a determined prophet from the trans-Jordan by the name of Elijah, was able finally to thwart Jezebel's plans.

The background material we have of Elijah is very sketchy. He seems to have come from the rather remote village of Tishbe in Gilead. Interestingly enough, the area was populated by sheepherders, not farmers.

Like most prophets of his time, Elijah felt that his commission to preach came directly from God. Whether or not his emergence to prominence coincided with the. expansion of Baalism can only be surmised. All we know for sure is that he was a fierce partisan for the old religion. Indeed, his very name advertised his convictions. It meant, literally, "Ja(weh) is God."

Elijah sensed, as seemingly no one else of his time, the danger in the encroaching Baalism. He saw its simultaneous religious attractiveness and shallowness. He recognized its inherent social and political deficiencies. Above all he realized that the basic reason for its spreading popularity lay with the queen. Jezebel was the principal enemy.

Elijah took up his cause against incredible odds. He had neither money, nor arms, nor influence.

Yet, the verdict of history is that in Elijah Jezebel met her match. Her tenacity did not match his. Her zeal did not burn so brightly.

All alone Elijah out-fought, out-argued, out-maneuvered Jezebel and her eight-hundred-plus religious henchmen. He denounced the religion of Baal in the cities and the hamlets, from the heights and from the valleys. He fought history with bigotry, and determined to go to any lengths to save Israel from religious apostasy.

Do we, then, detect elements of fanaticism in Elijah himself? We most certainly do! By any standard, Elijah was a fanatic; or perhaps, more accurately, a counter-fanatic. Whether or not Elijah would have been so fanatical in the absence of a Jezebel provides us with an interesting bit of speculation, though nothing more.

The struggle between Elijah and Jezebel reached its initial peak, so to speak, at the well-known contest on Mount Carmel. There a crowd of Israelites had gathered to witness a confrontation of the two religions.

Then Elijah said to the people, "I am the only prophet of the LORD still left, but there are four hundred and fifty prophets of Baal. Bring two bulls; let them choose one for themselves, cut it up and lay it on the wood without setting fire to it, and I will prepare the other and lay it on the wood without setting fire to it. You shall invoke your god by name and I will invoke the LORD by name; and the god who answers by fire, he is God." And all the people shouted their approval.

                                                              —I Kings 18:22–24

The narrative which follows is a masterpiece of dramatic religious polemic. One can almost visualize the prophets of Baal in their gorgeous vestments howling for the attention of their god. To one side stands the stern, aloof prophet from Tishbe. His attire, by comparison, is severe. They are the garments of a shepherd.

As Elijah watches the pagan ritual rise to a peak of religious frenzy, he takes to taunting its participants:

> At midday Elijah mocked them: "Call louder, for he is a god; it may be he is deep in thought, or engaged, or on a journey; or he may have gone to sleep and must be woken up." They cried still louder and, as was their custom, gashed themselves with swords and spears until the blood ran. All afternoon they raved and ranted till the hour of the regular sacrifice, but still there was no sound, no answer, no sign of attention.
>
> —I Kings 18:27–29

Note the contrast in ritual atmosphere when Elijah's turn comes!

> Then Elijah said to all the people, "Come here to me." They all came, and he repaired the altar of the LORD which had been torn down. He took twelve stones, one for each tribe of the sons of Jacob, the man named Israel by the word of the LORD. With these stones he built an altar in the name of the LORD; he dug a trench round it big enough to hold two measures of seed; he arranged the wood, cut up the bull and laid it on the wood. Then he said, "Fill four jars with water and pour it on the whole-offering and on the wood." They did so, and he said, "Do it again." They did it again, and he said, "Do it a third time." They did it a third time, and the water ran all round the altar and even filled the trench.
>
> —I Kings 18:30–35

Elijah's prayer, by comparison to the frantic cries of the prophets of Baal, is calm and rational. "Lord God of Abraham, of Isaac, and of Israel, let it be known today that thou art God in Israel . . ."

> Then the fire of the LORD fell. It consumed the whole-offering, the wood, the stones, and the earth, and licked up the water in the trench. When all the people saw it, they fell prostrate and cried, "The LORD is God, the LORD is God."
>
> —I Kings 18:38–39

The answer to Elijah's prayer, however, does not provide either justification or, indeed, explanation for what followed. What is referred to is the massacre of the prophets of Baal.

In dealing with this outrage one is left with certain conjectures. For example, did this occasion provide Elijah with an opportunity to lay blame for the disastrous drought on the assembled representatives of Baal and Asherah? Were the people then whipped into a murderous rage which ended in the slaughter of these foreign clergy? One cannot know. But the theory is tempting.

Whatever the reasons, whatever the justifications, Elijah's victory was short-lived. If he imagined that he had won certain debating points with Jezebel by wiping out her clerical advisers, he was badly mistaken. It is always a mistake to underestimate the resolve of a fanatic. Fanatics have immense resources for warding off the consequences of minor setbacks.

Jezebel's response to the obliteration of her retinue of prophets was not capitulation. No indeed! She responded instead with cold rage. There went out a little note to Elijah which read:

> "The gods do the same to me and more, unless by this time tomorrow I have taken your life as you took theirs."
>
> —I Kings 19:2

It was enough to send Elijah scurrying off to Hebron. There he remained in hiding until the unspeakable incident involving the seizure of Naboth's vineyard sent him storming back into the fray.

The story of Naboth and his point-blank refusal to sell his ancestral vineyard to King Ahab need not be recounted here. The reader is referred to I Kings, chapter 21. That Ahab should sulk over Naboth's rejection of his offer is understandable. In Israel there was no other recourse. Property rights were inviolable. Even the king was obliged to respect them.

But can Jezebel be excused for her lack of comprehension in the matter? Can she be excused for her calculated effort to frame Naboth and bring about his death so that the king could claim the property?

To some extent we are obliged to answer these questions in the affirmative. Jezebel, it must be remembered, was raised in a society where the rights of the king were absolute. In all probability she could not imagine how a vassal like Naboth had the right, much less the temerity, to refuse to turn over his vineyard to the king. That was not the way things were run back in Phoenicia.

Here again we see Jezebel's ideas running counter to those of the country in which she had come to live. Moreover, her fanatic rigidity apparently kept her from making the slightest effort to understand the reasons for a political philosophy differing from her own. One sees in Jezebel only a compulsive determination to turn Israel into a carbon copy of Phoenicia both religiously and politically.

Interestingly, the two characteristics bear on one another. Politics reflect religion, and vice versa. The religious dissimilarities which existed between Phoenicia and Israel had definite political consequences. In the case at hand it might be pointed out that the religion of Baal tended to support the notion of unchecked monarchism, while that of Jahweh tended to oppose it.

Why was this so? There is not space here to develop this matter in any detail. Let it suffice to point out that in Phoenicia the king was regarded as a sacred figure who, in the hierarchy of the cosmos, occupied a place between the gods and men.

Israel, on the contrary, with its uncompromising monotheism, with its firm conviction that there was no divine hierarchy immanent in the created order, that there was only one Creator God, and all the rest, including kings, were creatures, was religiously prevented from regarding the king as being anything more than a mere sinful man who, like all men, stood under the judgment of God. It is no exaggeration to say that of all the countries of the Near East at this time, only Israel had kings who were regularly berated by their religious spokesmen. One cannot imagine, for example, an Egyptian temple priest denouncing a Pharaoh as Elijah denounced Ahab!

In short, Israel's theological background endowed the nation with a kind of incipient democracy. And this Jezebel could not—or would not—understand.

The point being made here lends credence to the sequel to the disgraceful and illegal seizure of Naboth's vineyard. Ahab is pictured walking through the vineyard, gloating over his ill-got possession when, seemingly out of nowhere, Elijah appears, righteous fury written all over his face.

Ahab said to Elijah, "Have you found me, my enemy?" "I have found you," he said, "because you have sold yourself to do what is wrong in the eyes of the LORD. I will bring disaster upon you; I will sweep you away and destroy every mother's son of the house of Ahab in Israel. . . ." When Ahab heard this, he rent his clothes, put on sackcloth and fasted; he lay down in his sackcloth and went about muttering to himself.

—I Kings 21:20–21, 27

Jezebel must have been surprised to see her husband carrying on so. Ethbaal, her father, she may have thought, would have made short work of any religious functionary who dared to cross him.

"WHATSOEVER A MAN SOWETH . . ."

One of the major liabilities of fanaticism is its persistence. It is like a hard pesticide, a DDT which after fifty years has lost little of its toxicity and comes back to bedevil people in strange and unexpected ways. Consider, for example, the case of Northern Ireland.

Another problem with fanaticism is its fecundity. Fanaticism breeds quickly and spreads rapidly. Its presence in one person perpetuates a like fanaticism in others. And so it grows like a cancer until the inevitably tragic denouement.

What came of Jezebel's fanaticism?

For a time, nothing. During most of Ahab's reign life in Israel went on as usual. An onlooker would have said that Israel looked as prosperous as ever.

But the cancer was within. From the events which developed later, it is evident that religious feelings gradually began to get out of control.

The last chapter of Jezebel's life opened with the death of her husband on the battlefield of Ramoth Gilead. His son, Ahaziah, ruled Israel only a short time before he was killed in an accidental fall. Another of Ahab and Jezebel's sons, Jehoram, followed Ahaziah to the throne.

That old nemesis of Jezebel, Elijah, also disappeared from the scene. His prophetic mantle was now around the shoulders of a man named Elisha.

Of the major characters of the story, only Jezebel remained. She was an old woman now, living mostly in the

company of her memories—a mingling of regrets and satis-
factions. Still she would never know the peace to which
some elderly people are heir. The seeds of fanaticism which
she had sown were now ripening. They would soon bear
one hundredfold.

The instrument of that bitter harvest was a man by the
name of Jehu. Of his background we know very little. Somehow, considering the career to follow, it does not seem
important. What is important to know about Jehu is that
he is one of the most callous, blood-thirsty fanatics to be
found in the pages of the Bible. Beside him, Jezebel and
Elijah almost seem like a pair of Rotarians.

From every indication, Jehu was the sort who relished
killing in the service of what he regarded as religious truth.
He was squarely in the Torquemada tradition. Not that
there was anything new about that, of course. Slaughtering
people in the name of deity is one of the most venerable
of human institutions. Cain, in fact, started it all by killing
his brother over a religious difference of opinion. Jehu, unfortunately, was not the last of this particular line either.
His followers over the years have been legion. There are,
in fact, many Jehus in the world today.

Jehu was one of King Jehoram's army generals. He was
involved in the static warfare along the Syrian border when
word came to him that he could count on support from
certain religious leaders if he were to attempt to overthrow
the house of Ahab.

Sensing that the time was ripe, Jehu took immediate action. He remained in Ramoth Gilead only long enough to
ensure the allegiance of the other military commanders.

Then, driving furiously for Jezreel where the injured Jehoram was recuperating from battle wounds, Jehu urged his
horses to the limit of their endurance so as to arrive before
any possible warning.

There, in as cold-blooded an act of treachery as can be imagined, Jehu murdered the defenseless Jehoram and, for good measure, the visiting king of Judah (named Ahaziah, but not to be confused with the previous king of Israel).

The watchman standing on the watch-tower in Jezreel saw Jehu and his troop approaching and called out, "I see a troop of men." Then Jehoram said, "Fetch a horseman and send to find out if they come peaceably." The horseman went to meet him and said, "The king asks, 'Is it peace?'" Jehu said, "Peace? What is peace to you? Fall in behind me." Thereupon the watchman reported, "The messenger has met them but he is not coming back." A second horseman was sent; when he met them, he also said, "The king asks, 'Is it peace?'" "Peace?" said Jehu. "What is peace to you? Fall in behind me." Then the watchman reported, "He has met them but he is not coming back. The driving is like the driving of Jehu son of Nimshi, for he drives furiously." "Harness my chariot," said Jehoram. They harnessed it, and Jehoram king of Israel and Ahaziah king of Judah went out each in his own chariot to meet Jehu, and met him by the plot of Naboth of Jezreel. When Jehoram saw Jehu, he said, "Is it peace, Jehu?" But he replied, "Do you call it peace while your mother Jezebel keeps up her obscene idol-worship and monstrous sorceries?" Jehoram wheeled about and fled, crying out to Ahaziah, "Treachery, Ahaziah!" Jehu seized his bow and shot Jehoram between the shoulders; the arrow pierced his heart and he sank down in his chariot.

—II Kings 9:17–25

Jezebel was the next to go.

At some time later—we cannot know the time sequence here, we know only that Jezebel had already become aware of her son's assassination—Jehu arrived at the residence of the queen.

Jezebel had made no attempt to escape. On the contrary, she had carefully prepared herself for her inevitable death.

Arrayed in her finest clothing, adorned with her finest cos-
metics, Jezebel awaited Jehu. When he arrived, she greeted
him from her window. She showed no fear. She did not
beg for mercy. Rather, she coolly insulted Jehu. She did not
even call him by his right name. She used the name of
Zimri, that of one of the more loathsome thugs in Israel's
history.

Jehu came to Jezreel. Now Jezebel had heard what had
happened; she had painted her eyes and dressed her hair, and
she stood looking down from a window. As Jehu entered the
gate, she said, "Is it peace, you Zimri, you murderer of your
master?" He looked up at the window and said, "Who is on my
side, who?" Two or three eunuchs looked out, and he said,
"Throw her down." They threw her down, and some of her
blood splashed on to the wall and the horses, which trampled
her underfoot. Then he went in and ate and drank. "See to
this accursed woman," he said, "and bury her; for she is a
king's daughter." But when they went to bury her they found
nothing of her but the skull, the feet, and the palms of the
hands. . . .

—II Kings 9:30–36

It is indicative of the character of Jehu that he should
follow his brutal act with a bout of feasting and drinking.
For Jehu, however, this was merely the beginning. The blood-
baths soon followed. The members of Ahab's family were
exterminated first. The Baal worshipers followed. After all,
what better way of eliminating political and religious opposition?

Jehu became the next king of Israel. In his effort to
establish a dynasty he succeeded. Yet he failed too. Israel
became so weakened by the blood-letting that the country
quickly degenerated into a third-rate power, a virtual colony
of Damascus.

Thus, what was begun by a fanatic was concluded by an archfanatic. And so the story ends.

AND SO FORTH

Yet in one sense the story of Jezebel does not end. The names change. There comes a different locale, a different set of circumstances, different ideologies, different points in history. But the story goes on.

In ways great and small, fanaticism continues to exact its toll among men. One hears its echoes today in the renewed cries for "holy war" in the Middle East. Its effects are discernible in charred ruins in Northern Ireland. We feel its power in the invidious zeal of those committed to the religion of communism, not forgetting that of those who are similarly committed to the religion of anti-communism.

Even on a small scale, fanaticism sows the seeds of discord and confusion. For example, in our area of upstate New York just before Easter of this year, a minister of a nearby church took a paid advertisement in a local paper. And what was his Holy Week message? It was the good news that anyone who believed that Jesus was crucified on a Friday rather than a Wednesday was without any question bound to flames of eternal perdition.

Just where this clergyman dredged up this peculiar theory is anyone's guess. Why it could possibly make any difference is a question which only a fanatic could answer.

Again, as these pages were being written, a woman spoke of being hounded to the point of emotional collapse by a person who, in the name of friendship and an extremely conservative interpretation of the Christian faith, set about destroying her religious beliefs in the apparent hope of converting her to something better. When these efforts failed, this woman was informed that she had a spirit of the devil in her.

Fanaticism is one of the two great distortions of Christian commitment, the other being its opposite, indifference. The Christian is obliged to walk a razor's edge between the one and the other. He must possess warmth and conviction without supposing that he has a corner on God's truth. He must be restrained and tolerant without turning spiritually cold or impassive.

Of the two extremes, fanaticism is easily the worst. The situation at Laodicea is much to be preferred to the presence of a Jezebel. Fanaticism's potential for violence, for injustice, for inhumanity makes it one of the most profoundly anti-religious phenomena to be found in human experience.

The point is illustrated in an incident related by the late Dean Church. He tells of once seeing the words, "The yre of man wyrketh not the justice of God" scratched on the stone walls of a guardroom attached to one of the summer houses of the Medicis. Church surmised that the inscription was written there by some lonely English mercenary in response to the horrors of the fanaticism of the latter part of the sixteenth century.

Church went on to quote the more familiar translation of these words from the Epistle of St. James: "The wrath of man worketh not the righteousness of God," and concluded, "No, indeed. The wrath of man may be God's scourge and punishment."

VII NEHEMIAH:
BUILDER OF WALLS

No man whose testicles have been crushed or whose organ has
been severed shall become a member of the assembly of the
LORD.

—Deuteronomy 23:1

THE GROTESQUE FIGURE IN THE TEMPLE

One day, somewhere around the year 443 B.C., a man entered the precincts of the temple in Jerusalem bearing a
scroll in his hand.

The various worshipers and officials in the outer courts
doubtless turned and stared at the man as he passed by.
This was not because he was finely dressed, although undoubtedly he was more finely arrayed than anyone around.
The quality of the fabric of his cloak, the cut of it, the
workmanship, were not the sort of things one often saw in
the Jerusalem of that day.

Nor was he a cynosure because of his high governmental
status, though this was his in an unusual degree. The man
had just completed a twelve-year term as governor of Judah.
But more importantly, he was the personal cupbearer of
Artaxerxes, the Persian king. It was a position of intimacy,

hence of immense power. No doubt he carried or wore
some badge of his office on his person, and was accompanied by a small retinue of servants and bodyguards.

Still it was neither for his finery nor his high office that
people stared at him. Rather it was because for all this he
remained a grotesque figure still—overlarge, bloated even, a
round beardless face, given to a shambling walk, and, when
turning to give orders to his servants, speaking in a high
and unmistakably feminine voice.

Eunuchs, for such this man was, were not unknown in
Judah. But they were rare enough to provoke a certain
revulsion in those who encountered them. However rich or
prestigious a eunuch might be, he was an oddity and a
cripple in the eyes of a people who measured their real
wealth in the number of children they possessed—sons especially.

Moreover, the process of emasculation was a pagan practice. For a people who believed that God had set man
into the world in order to be fruitful and multiply, castra-
tion was regarded as an unthinkable disfigurement. For this
reason, a neutered male was traditionally denied any place
in the congregation of Israel, as witnesses the text above.

If the man who entered the temple precincts were something less than a man, the building he approached was
something less than a temple. It was a shadow of the
splendid structure erected by Solomon as a royal chapel
and cultic center for all Israel. Solomon's ornate edifice had
been destroyed during the devastation of Jerusalem by the
Chaldean king, Nebuchadnezzar. Its gold and silver vessels,
its metal and wood ornamentations, its ivory panels and
costly embroidered draperies had been taken off to Babylon,
and the structure itself torn apart.

It remained a ruin for nearly three generations. Then the
Persian regime replaced that of the Chaldeans, and there
came about some broad new policies regarding captive peoples.

Under an edict of Cyrus the Great in 539, deportees were allowed to return to their own lands and rebuild, if they so desired, the shrines of their various religions.

Under the provisions of this edict, a reconstruction of the Jerusalem temple was begun under the leadership of a man by the name of Zerubbabel.

Work progressed slowly. The people were poor and demoralized. Often they gave up the task, only to be stung into action once more by the harsh words of prophets like Haggai:

Is it a time for you to live in your own well-roofed houses, while this house lies in ruins?

—Haggai 1:4

In time the so-called "second temple" was finished. The doors were reopened. The sacrifices were begun again. But the structure, though it was the same size and general description of Solomon's before it, must have been a vastly inferior affair. In time Herod would try to win Jewish support by building a proper temple, which gives some idea of the second temple's condition.

So they were quite a pair, this grotesque man and this less than imposing religious building.

We can make but a slightly informed guess as to what followed. How far into the inner portions of the temple the man proceeded cannot be known. Perhaps he remained in the outer court and had one of his Jewish servants take the scroll inside. Perhaps he went inside and placed the scroll before the Altar of Burnt Offering. He may even have placed it on the steps leading to the Holy Place, there to be carried inside by a priest and laid upon the Altar of Incense.

Whatever the ceremonial, the presentation of that scroll amounted to an offering of a most poignant nature. For it was what scholars generally believe to have been a "me-

morial inscription," that is, a document by which a man hoped
to be remembered after he died.

To understand the poignancy of this particular memorial
inscription, it must be understood that at this time the
religion of Israel had no real doctrine of life after death.
Because the Hebraic tradition had been driven by what
one observer has described as its "relentless secularity" into
denying all mythical concepts of an afterlife, the only hope
a man could have for survival after death in those days
was through his progeny. Children were the means by which
a man lived on after his demise.

Thus there was no misfortune quite so devastating in
Hebrew culture as childlessness, no condition so blessed as
an abundance of children.

> Like arrows in the hand of a fighting man
>   are the sons of a man's youth.
> Happy is the man
>   who has his quiver full of them;
> such men shall not be put to shame
>   when they confront their enemies in court.
>   —Psalm 127:4–5

The eunuch in the temple, it goes without saying, was
beyond any such hope. There would be no son to remember *him!* No child would convey *his* name to the next generation! No grandchildren would cherish *his* memory! No gen-
ealogy list, so important in the minds of the ancient Israelites,
would enshrine *his* name!

And so it was he came to the temple bringing what he
must have conceived as being a very poor alternative to a
family. All he possessed in place of many sons was a
written account of his actions during a critical period in
the history of the children of Israel. This would have to
take the place of progeny in his bid for a name which would

be remembered by the people of God. "Remember for my good, O God," he wrote, "all this that I have done for this people."

Having made his offering, he turned about and left the temple in order to attend to the many duties which besieged him. Like Origen, the self-emasculated Biblical scholar of the third century A.D., the lack of virility in no way hindered the man's industriousness.

We surmise that the scroll was afterwards taken by a Levite and deposited in the temple archives. There it remained quite forgotten for a very long time. Then, some two hundred years later—and this is also a surmise—the scroll was chanced upon by a man known to scholars only as the "Chronicler."

At the time, the Chronicler was in the process of putting together an account of the reestablishment of the religion of Israel after the Captivity. Because he was very favorably disposed toward a strict Judaism, the Chronicler gave special emphasis to the rebuilding of the temple and the fortifications which protected it. The scroll he found provided him with exactly what he needed, for it contained a firsthand account of the rebuilding of the walls of Jerusalem.

The memorial inscription was edited slightly. Certain other documents were dovetailed into the narrative. Through this process the memoir came, in time, to achieve a place in that preeminent book, the Holy Bible.

It was in such a roundabout manner that the prayer of that grotesque man in the temple on that day many years before, the prayer that he be remembered for his part in the refortification of Jerusalem, came to be answered. For the name of that eunuch, the cupbearer of the Persian king Artaxerxes I, and the governor of Judah for twelve years, was Nehemiah. It is his memorial inscription which makes up most of the sixteenth book of the Old Testament, the book which bears his name.

NEHEMIAH'S STORY

He was a man of kind and just nature and most anxious to
serve his countrymen, and he left the walls of Jerusalem as his
eternal monument.

—Josephus

Nehemiah's story begins in Susa, a city beyond the Tigris
River, situated in what is present-day Iraq. It was here
that the kings of the Persian empire kept their summer
palaces. The incumbent was Artaxerxes I, grandson of Darius.

Nehemiah happened to be one of those deported Judeans
who, through ability, or chance, or a combination of the
two, had risen to the position of king's cupbearer. It was
a position of great trust. The cupbearer was an intimate of
the king. His job it was to serve the king his food, more
particularly to taste it before the king did, a precaution
against poisoning. The confidence placed in Nehemiah was
all the greater when it is remembered that the king's own
father, Xerxes, was assassinated by one of his attendants.

Depictions of cupbearers appear in many of the artistic
renditions which survive from these days, such as those
that appear in the friezes of Darius' palace. They are shown
with their towels and fly whisks, their golden goblets borne
aloft. Invariably they appear beardless, for it seems to have
been a universal custom that such intimate servants of
the court, with their ready access to the harem and the
queen's chambers, were emasculated. The practice was still
alive in the time of Christ, for even Herod the Great had
a eunuch cupbearer.

Servants of the king though they may have been, cup-
bearers must have wielded immense personal power. Holders
of the king's trust, they were the closest to his ear. Their

favor must have been curried by small and great alike. Without doubt the king regularly sought their advice. As the opening scenes of the book of Nehemiah indicate, cup-bearers were treated with considerable familiarity, even affection, by the king.

Thus it is not at all surprising that a household servant of the king should have been appointed to a twelve-year term as governor of Judah. Quite the reverse! In respect to genuine power, the appointment may have been more of a demotion than otherwise.

As Nehemiah tells the story in his memorial inscription, he was surprised one day by the visit of a brother. The brother apparently had just come from Judah. Being a devout Jew, Nehemiah inquired of his brother the condition of the holy city, Jerusalem.

More than likely he expected a favorable report. After all, many of the exiled Judeans had long ago returned to their homeland under the edict of Cyrus. Zerubbabel's reconstruction of the temple was long since an accomplished fact. So far as Nehemiah was concerned, Jerusalem was well on its way toward total rehabilitation and the fulfill-ment of such prophecies as those of Jeremiah nearly two hundred years before.

These are the words of the LORD: You say of this place, "It is in ruins, and neither man nor beast lives in the cities of Judah or in the streets of Jerusalem. It is all a waste, inhabited by neither man nor beast." Yet in this place shall be heard once again the sounds of joy and gladness, the voice of the bride-groom and the bride; here too shall be heard voices shouting, "Praise the LORD of Hosts, for he is good, for his love endures for ever," as they offer praise and thanksgiving in the house of the LORD. For I will restore the fortunes of the land as once they were. This is the word of the LORD.

—Jeremiah 33:10-11

To his sorrow, Nehemiah learned that the situation in
Jerusalem was far from good. The city remained largely
uninhabited. The returning Judeans found themselves a dis-
criminated-against minority. The walls surrounding Israel's
most precious shrines remained in a state of disrepair.

The news desolated Nehemiah. He took to his knees and
began a period of fasting, mourning and prayer.

It was not long before the king observed Nehemiah's
great distress.

"Why do you look so unhappy? You are not ill; it can be
nothing but unhappiness."

—Nehemiah 2:2

Nehemiah's answer was the shrewd retort of a courtier.
In effect he told the king that the tombs of his ancestors
were endangered. To Artaxerxes, a man much concerned
at the time with the building of his own burial place, such a
thought was unbearable. That the bones of his personal cupbearer's ancestors were in danger of being desecrated was a
monstrous notion, and Artaxerxes was only too glad to dispatch Nehemiah to Jerusalem with the necessary funds and
authority to set things right.

After a long journey, Nehemiah arrived in Jerusalem
with his "escort of army officers with cavalry." There he
presented the royal documents which set out his unquestion-
able authority.

As might have been expected, Nehemiah was hardly
greeted with smiles by the existing administrators. He
aroused their immediate envy and suspicion. For a long
time they had exercised a hegemony over the Jerusalem
area, and had profited from the city's continued state of
disrepair. The advent of Nehemiah did not auger well for
them.

For the first three days Nehemiah did nothing. He bode

his time, perhaps hoping that his potential adversaries would put him down for one more lackadaisical eunuch. Then one night, which for sheer adventure rivals any in the Bible, Nehemiah slipped out from his quarters and made a secret investigation of the walls of Jerusalem.

It cannot be doubted that every effort was made to conceal the investigation. It was of the utmost importance that none of Nehemiah's enemies learn of his intentions until it was too late to do anything about them.

One can almost picture Nehemiah's small reconnaissance party moving in and out of the shadows created by the combination of bright moonlight and towering ruins, fearing that each dislodged and clattering stone behind them might have been caused by some lurking spy.

When Nehemiah had fully assessed the nature of the damage to the walls and their gates, he returned to his dwelling. It does not say so, but we can assume that he spent a great deal of time in the days to follow formulating a plan of repair. He then called together an assembly of the leading Jews in the area. He explained what needed doing and how it was to be done.

From what followed, it must be acknowledged that for the ability to organize and motivate men, Nehemiah was a rarity, even a genius. The manner in which he divided his work is indicative of the man's outstanding leadership. Each section of the wall was assigned to a certain group or family of Jews. No doubt Nehemiah initiated a great spirit of competition among them. Each tried to outdo the other. Yet all worked for a common goal.

Further, we are told that under Nehemiah's leadership all of the old, customary cowardice vanished. For the first time in living memory, the Jews of the area refused to be intimidated by the non-Judean majority. The threat of armed intervention was met by the avowed determination to fight, if need be, so that the work of reconstructing the walls could be finished.

The bare statistics found in the Bible witness to Nehemiah's remarkable organizational and motivational abilities. This man was able to accomplish in fifty-two days what the resettled Jews had been unable to do in fifty-two years and more. In less than two months the job was done.

It is of considerable importance, in understanding Nehemiah's venture, to comprehend the extent and significance of the rebuilding of the walls of Jerusalem.

First, the walls rebuilt under Nehemiah's leadership did not encompass all of the Jerusalem of that day. Nehemiah did not have it in mind to build a fortified city, as some of his opponents claimed. These particular walls did not extend much beyond the sacred center of the city—which is to say that portion which enclosed the temple and the ground which had once been the site of David's palace (in other words, the height on the eastern flank of the city known as Mount Zion). This part of Jerusalem was an elongated ridge immediately west of the Kidron depression, across from which rose the Mount of Olives. Its circumference was not much more than two and one-half miles.

Also it must be stated that the walls had not been totally demolished during the destruction of Jerusalem. Rather they had been severely breached in several places, and subject to erosion and collapse in others. Most heavily damaged were the gates, which had been made of wood and subsequently put to the torch. Still the job was one of considerable magnitude, not to say audacity.

The underlying purpose of Nehemiah's reconstruction must have been clear to all. What Nehemiah had in mind was to reestablish a Jewish identity. He was not wall-building for wall-building's sake. Nehemiah's intention was both to define and isolate the religious wellsprings of Judaism. By enclosing the sacred precincts of the old royal palace and the temple, by making it fully clear who was entitled to access to these shrines and who was not, Nehemiah meant to emphasize once more the particular place which the Jewish people occupied both in the world and in the sight of God. Hence the term often associated with Nehemiah is that of "particularism."

Once a person grasps this aspect of Nehemiah's task, he can begin to understand the ire which the rebuilding of the walls of Jerusalem aroused in many quarters.

In his memorial inscription, Nehemiah singled out three of his principal adversaries. These were Sanballat the Horonite, Tobiah the Ammonite, and Geshem the Arab.

The opposition of these men to Nehemiah is not difficult to fathom. As a Samaritan, Sanballat felt that his credentials as a worshiper of Jahweh, the God of Israel, were quite impeccable. The Samaritans had filled the vacuum left by the annihilation of the so-called "ten lost tribes of Israel" in the eighth century B.C. In time they began to look upon themselves as an Israelite remnant.

But to the Judeans the Samaritans were not Israelites. They were tainted Jews at best, and pagan colonists and usurpers at worst.

Quite naturally the Samaritans resented such treatment. Further, they had suffered a grievous blow to their religious self-esteem when, several generations before, their offer to help Zerubbabel with the rebuilding of the temple had been refused. At that time they were rebuffed as being something less than Jewish, and hence ineligible to participate in Jewish worship. During the time of Nehemiah the split between Samaritan and Jew would widen until, some years later, the Samaritans would construct a rival temple on Mount Gerizim outside Schechem.

Sanballat viewed Nehemiah's project with any number of negative sentiments. Certainly he did not wish to have his own political autonomy jeopardized by the reestablishment

of a strong Judean state. Nor did he want the easygoing
Persian authorities riled up against all minorities by the
defensive posturings of one.

But among these more practical considerations, there still
remained the matter of religious exclusivism. It must have
been a galling experience for Sanballat and his fellow countrymen to be excluded from certain religious shrines to
which they felt entitled. No one likes to be told, either by
words or walls, that his religion is intrinsically inferior.

Sanballat's allies, Tobiah the Ammonite and Geshem the
Arab, were men with similar complaints. Their authority had
been granted by the Persian government. Their religion
was a mild form of Jahwism. Nehemiah's walls had the
effect of compromising both.

The three used ridicule and threat, warning and treachery in their campaign against Nehemiah. They even attempted to lure him away from the city for a negotiating
session, one which Nehemiah felt would end with a knife
in his back.

Nehemiah's response was to give them no more than wary
attention and press on with the work at hand. In a remarkably short time the walls were rebuilt and the gates repaired.

This done, Nehemiah set about putting together a mammoth ceremony of consecration.

At the dedication of the wall of Jerusalem they sought out the
Levites in all their settlements, and brought them to Jerusalem
to celebrate the dedication with rejoicing, with thanksgiving
and song, to the accompaniment of cymbals, lutes, and harps.
. . . Then I brought the leading men of Judah up on to the
city wall, and appointed two great choirs to give thanks. . . .
A great sacrifice was celebrated that day, and they all rejoiced
because God had given them great cause for rejoicing; the
women and children rejoiced with them. And the rejoicing in
Jerusalem was heard a long way off.

—Nehemiah 12:27, 31, 43

It takes little imagination to visualize the emotional response of the people to this great occasion. How their hearts must have soared when they realized that their holy city had been restored to them!

> I rejoiced when they said to me,
>   "Let us go to the house of the LORD."
> Now we stand within your gates,
>   O Jerusalem:
> Jerusalem that is built to be a city
>   where people come together in unity;
> to which the tribes resort, the tribes of the LORD,
>   to give thanks to the LORD himself,
>   the bounden duty of Israel.
> For in her are set the thrones of justice
>   the thrones of the house of David.
> Pray for the peace of Jerusalem:
>   "May those who love you prosper;
> peace be within your ramparts
>   and prosperity in your palaces."
> For the sake of these my brothers and my friends,
>   I will say, "Peace be within you."
> For the sake of the house of the LORD our God
>   I will pray for your good.
>   —Psalm 122

The task of rebuilding the walls was for Nehemiah only a beginning. Certain other walls—walls of the mind, walls of the spirit—had to be torn down, and others built up.

Nehemiah saw the necessity for a new feeling of Jewish brotherhood. He set out stern laws against the custom of usury which had hitherto set Jew against Jew.

He reinstituted laws against the profaning of the temple and the sabbath.

He realized that Jerusalem would have to be quickly resettled by his own people if it were to assume a Jewish character. So he required that one Jew in every ten living in the near countryside take up quarters in the ruined city.

He inveighed against the custom of intermarriage between the Jews and their Semitic neighbors, and in so doing further alienated the Sanballat faction.

More positively, he set a model for theocratic government by maintaining standards of utter integrity in the administration of his territory.

When it was all over, when Nehemiah returned for the last time to his post in the court of Artaxerxes, he could look back on a record of incredible accomplishment—indeed, an accomplishment so great that throughout the rest of his life he would never have to fear the kind of report which had sent him to Jerusalem in the first place.

Doubtless he often wished he could settle in his beloved Jerusalem himself. Even more he must have yearned for a son to bear his patrimony in a living succession down through the ages.

But this had been denied Nehemiah. All that he would leave behind were the rebuilt walls and all that went with it—a city awakened to a new corporate life, a religious revival, a new hope among the people of God.

And, of course, there was that scroll!

We might imagine Nehemiah in his old age thinking about that scroll, wondering if it were being taken care of, wondering if perhaps a chance fire had destroyed it, or if a family of mice had eaten it; wondering if it might lie fallow forever—forgotten and unread.

Whatever his conjectures about the fate of that scroll, we may be sure that he never imagined that his memorial inscription would come to be a part of the sacred writings of Israel, that it would take its place alongside the Law of Moses, the Psalms of David, the writings of the prophets. But his prayer was answered, so that never, till the end of time, will his name or deeds be forgotten.

THE PERILS OF WALL-BUILDING

"The LORD loves the gates of Zion"
—Psalm 87:1

The story of Nehemiah seems curiously out of joint for our times. Wall-builders are not apt to be popular figures these days. Given the prevailing temperament of the time, few could be persuaded of the necessity, much less the rightness of Nehemiah's task. His walls seem merely divisive, merely faction-makers. They are likely to be viewed as an extremely arbitrary means of excluding one group of people from another.

Nehemiah is often held responsible for the Jewish-Samaritan split. Consequently, some may regard him as an appropriate hero for such ages as that of the Reformation, but hardly our own.

Still, in judging Nehemiah, we must not fail to judge ourselves. What is to be made of the counter-tendencies of our own age? Are they quite beyond all criticism? Is there nothing to be said on Nehemiah's behalf? Has the story of Nehemiah nothing to offer the twentieth century?

The fact is that men seem doomed to live either in wall-building or wall-breaking times. Either there is a general disposition to erect and maintain the various walls of mind and matter which divide people, or there is the contrary disposition to tear them down and glory in their destruction.

Surely we live in a period of wall-breaking in our days. Indeed, there have been few periods in history so devoted to the shattering of walls as our own. At all levels of human life the old traditional walls have come tumbling down. Recently the pace has accelerated. The barriers seem to be coming down as suddenly and catastrophically as the walls of Jericho.

We can rejoice in the breaking down of many of these walls. Racial walls come instantly to mind. We have only recently become sensitized to the basic injustice of walls which arbitrarily divide one race from another. Many white people have become horrified to discover the humiliation and anger which the walls of prejudice and segregation create for those who are left on the outside.

Again, twenty years ago it would have been impossible to foresee the suddenness with which the walls dividing the churches of Christendom would be breached. The ecumenical movement was inching along in those days, and the prevailing sentiment of its leaders was that church unity was something which would not be seen in their times. Yet, on a practical, if not an organizational, level, an astonishing degree of Christian unity has been achieved in the past few years. For this we are also glad.

Once more, we can derive considerable satisfaction from the dissolution of the walls of nationalism. Much as people love their homelands, most have come to the thoughtful realization that the basic unity of all mankind is of considerably greater importance than any national identification. Persons today, especially the young, recognize the harm which can come of fanatical, belligerent nationalism. They know that the only hope for peace will come from a sense of amity and equality among nations.

Such an insight is one which even the warmest of patriots can no longer avoid. The unity of mankind matters more than its divisions. The point was beautifully made by one of the astronauts somewhere between the earth and the moon. As he looked out of the space capsule's porthole toward the glistening blue orb which floated tens of thousands of miles away from him through the vast spaces of the universe, he likened the planet Earth to a great spaceship which sheltered and sustained the one race of man.

We can hope that the walls described above have been dismantled for good, in every sense of the term. Yet there are other walls whose destruction in our times is much more open to question.

Without doubt, the rate at which the walls which surround, for example, the institution of marriage are being destroyed must make us pause and wonder. The relaxation of divorce laws, the increase in trial marriages, the phenomenon known as group marriage, the increase in temporary liaisons, casual parenthood and the like, have come about with unbelievable swiftness.

Despite the breezy reassurances of their advocates, we cannot fail to wonder what the long-range effect of these developments will be on children reared outside the walls of the traditional family structure.

Another instance of wall-breaking which gives many cause for alarm is the rapidity with which the walls dividing the sexes are crumbling before our eyes. The campus scene provides a number of instances: colleges traditionally all male or all female going coeducational, the doing away with almost all restrictions governing heterosexual behavior on the campus, the institution of "coed dorms," and so forth.

In other areas of society we find traditional male vocations being opened to women (and vice versa, as, for example, the increase in the number of male nurses).

Among the various churches the ordination of women has come to be a common practice. Even within the more traditional churches, like the Roman Catholic or Anglican, there is to be found considerable sentiment in favor of ordaining women to the priesthood. Even more astonishing, perhaps, is the fact that within Judaism there are women preparing to serve as rabbis, thus breaking a tradition some twenty-five hundred years old.

Other indications of the breaching of sexual walls are the ways in which men and women have begun to dress alike, groom alike, act alike. The term "unisex" has emerged to describe the phenomenon.

Codes of etiquette which once served to distinguish the role of men from that of women have all but disappeared. The sexual relationship itself has become increasingly casual. Men no longer seem afraid to assume the role of women, and even flaunt their homosexuality. Women begin to practice not only some of the traditionally masculine pastimes, but take over some of the less desirable male customs as well, such as the inclination to settle differences by force, or by freely and openly resorting to what was once referred to as "locker room language."

Even at the level of the individual self we have not been spared the wall-breaking tendencies of modern civilization. For example, much psychological energy is currently being poured into the breaking down of a person's "defenses." This process is almost universally and uncritically regarded as therapeutic. Conventional psychology abounds with terms which describe well-being as the absence of various inner and outer barriers. Thus the healthy person is the "open" person, or the "uninhibited" person. He is the one who is free from all "restraints" or "repressions."

In order to achieve a facile degree of "self-disclosure," people resort to sensitivity sessions, to training ("T") groups, to encounter groups. Some even hie themselves off to places like the Esalen Institute in California where they can really work at the business of divesting themselves of the walls which divide them from others.

All of which leads to the subject of public nudity—which can hardly be avoided in this context, for clothing is a form of walls. Indeed, what we wear is a very intricate means of self-protection. A person's dress both conceals and, in some measure, reveals the inner person, a fact which has been known intuitively by the great portrait artists of all times.

There are few more telling indications of the prevailing attitudes and opinions than current fashions. For this reason, the widespread toleration of public nudity, from see-through clothing in public places to stark nakedness in theatres and on the screen, must be regarded as more than an epidemic of lasciviousness. Similarly with the accompanying attitude that modesty is a form of prudishness or neurotic inhibition. The more profound significance lies in the areas of the wall-breaking tendencies outlined above.

These various instances of wall-breaking are but a few examples. There are many others which, no doubt, come to the reader's mind. What must be noted here, however, is the distinct possibility that this tendency has overreached itself. Soon there is likely to come a corrective reaction.

People can gleefully destroy the walls which surround them and dance on their ruins for only so long. Soon comes the somber realization that the walls which hemmed them in also protected them.

Walls are a necessity of life. Without them people soon begin to feel defenseless. They become oppressed by a feeling of chaos, and there is nothing a human being fears quite so much as chaos. Chaos turns to panic. Panicky people begin to wonder where they belong, or who they might be. Their identity begins to turn fluid. They grow terror-stricken, even dangerous.

Much "turning off" through the use of various drugs could be said to be caused by the loss of identity which has come about through the destruction of old, protective walls. Without them the world, for many, has become intolerably complex. People have found themselves faced with the alternative of escaping a chaotic world or going mad.

By the same token, the person whose life has remained bounded by the old walls of nation and tradition, who has

L.I.F.E. College Library
1100 Glendale Blvd.
Los Angeles, Calif. 90026

continued to feel secure within the boundaries of his religion, his culture, his society, his marriage, his sexual role, his vocation, would hardly be apt to go on a hallucinogenic trip. There is no compulsion to do so, for his world is comfortable and protective, and there is no need to escape it.

Within a generation or two, many of the walls which have been torn down in our times will begin to be raised once more. It would seem that further destruction is simply intolerable. The world has turned edgy. People have begun to learn through painful experience that humans cannot live without walls.

Having said as much, the story of Nehemiah takes on a considerable degree of currency. It was within a chaotic situation similar to our own that Nehemiah asserted himself. He suggested that it was time to build up the walls once more, and the people were only too glad to listen. They had lived among the ruins too long.

So they built the walls. They reinvigorated their religion. In the process they may have become exclusivistic, but it cannot be denied that a strong Judaism emerged from within those walls, a Judaism which survived the powerful on-slaughts of the period of Hellenization which was to come.

Postexilic Judaism, which in large measure derived its identity from Nehemiah's walls, survived a great period of testing intact. In so doing it remained to become the spiritual nurture of Jesus of Nazareth. It was also the religious founda-tion of every apostle and church leader of the formative period in the Church's life. Its Scriptures nourished the first Christians, its worship set an indelible mark upon the pat-terns of Christian worship, its theology informed the first faltering steps of Christian theology. For these reasons, and many others, the Christian should hesitate before heaping any cheap criticisms on Nehemiah or his objectives.

One final aspect of the matter must be pointed out on Nehemiah's behalf: namely that he himself was an outsider.

As a eunuch, he had no rightful place within the walls which he himself erected. Nehemiah knew something about the perils of wall-building. He must have realized their potentiality for divisiveness and injustice.

Would it be too fanciful to suggest that this may have been one of the reasons that Nehemiah concentrated so much effort on gates of those walls? Read his memoir! Note the amount of concern paid to the condition of the passages *through* those walls!

Perhaps Nehemiah wistfully hoped that there would someday be a gate for even such as himself into the inner courts of God—an idea which, whether he knew it or not, was already being affirmed by an unknown near-contemporary whose writings came to be appended to the book of Isaiah.

> The foreigner who has given his allegiance to the LORD must not say, "The LORD will keep me separate from his people for ever"; and the eunuch must not say, "I am nothing but a barren tree."

> —Isaiah 56:3

VIII RUTH:
THE REAL MEANING OF A STORY

Where truth in closest words shall fail
. . . truth embodied in a tale
shall enter in at lowly doors.

—Tennyson

In a general way, the purpose of a story in our modern, western civilization is primarily to entertain. When a person picks up a book of the short stories of Saki or John O'Hara or Somerset Maugham, he expects to be diverted. Perhaps he is tired after a long day at the office and wants to take his mind off his many responsibilities. Or a housewife might for a few moments desire to leave the world of dishes and laundry and the incessant importunities of children for a much more romantic environment.

Whatever the reason, what we ask of a story today is to be beguiled by a plot, or intrigued by skillful description and dialogue, or entranced by the author's insights into the vagaries of human nature.

Very few readers expect, or even desire, to be instructed by the stories they read. Students, occasionally, earnestly search for deep meanings in the literature they read; but most readers are content to drift along on the surface of the story. Indeed, many can become downright irritated if the storyteller lards his goods with too many messages.

It is of considerable importance to the reader of the Bible to understand that this attitude toward stories did not prevail in ancient times. Then the meaning of the story was fully as important as its entertainment value. The Biblical stories, most of which were told around nomadic campfires for many centuries before they were committed to writing, were as valued for the message they conveyed as their capacity to amuse.

To be sure they *were* expected to entertain. The listeners to those stories (it scarcely needs pointing out that very few were read in Old Testament times) fully expected to be interested by what they heard. Without a doubt the hearers would turn very grouchy if the story failed to hold their attention. Leslie Weatherhead, the British writer and preacher, has noted that where these ancient storytelling traditions continue to be maintained, in certain more primitive parts of Arab culture, a poor storyteller is apt to be hissed out of a tent by his disgruntled listeners.

The stories of the Biblical world, however, were expected to do far more than divert people. In those days, stories were one of the principal vehicles for the transmission of ideas. Religion and ethics, philosophy and history, heritage and tradition were customarily conveyed from tribe to tribe, and from generation to generation through means of stories.

Many of the stories were etiological in nature, which is to say they were "How come?" stories. They explained the origin of things—place names, customs, tribal characteristics and so forth. The establishment of nearly every shrine in the Old Testament is explained by some story or other.

More profoundly, these stories dealt with many of the queries put by primeval man to the unfathomable riddles of his existence. A rather simple illustration of this would have to do with the question of why people speak various lan-

guages, a question which continues to fascinate children especially. The answer provided by the story of the Tower of
Babel, with its implication that separation from God invariably results in a radical alienation among men, even to
the point of their inability to communicate with one another,
provided an extraordinarily thoughtful, not to mention theological, explanation of the phenomenon of language.

Most Christians today are rather ignorant of the extent to
which the stories of Israel were made to bear the religious
insights, the confessions and the basic convictions of the
people of God. To become aware of the numerous instances
and the serious purpose of the Biblical story would revolu-
tionize the reading of the Bible for many thousands of people. It would do so not only by releasing them from the
grip of historical positivism and its relentless question: "Did
it *really* happen?" It would also bring a measure of enjoy-
ment to the incredibly rich and beautiful means by which
the nation of Israel preserved its religious treasures.

It seems strange, perhaps, that the prevalence of the story
form in the Old Testament has not occurred to more people,
especially when it is recalled that Jesus himself conveyed the
bulk of his message through means of stories. It must be
acknowledged, however, that Jesus usually made it clear that
he was about to utilize that form of discourse known as a
parable, whereas the stories of the Old Testament seem to be
presented as actual facts (though our story of Ruth is an
exception).

Still, the original hearers were not confused by these stories, as we tend to be. It would be doubtful in the first place
that they so much as grasped the concept of factual history
as we know it. But willy-nilly, they did assume two attitudes
toward their stories which it would be well for the modern
Bible reader to remember.

First, they assumed that while what was being told was
based upon an actual event, it was a story still, hence subject

to all of the changes and distortions which the countless retellings of any story entails.

Second, unlike most of us, they assumed that the historical reliability of the story was of secondary importance. What counted was what the story *meant*. Such a concern was very much in accord with the Semitic turn of mind, which delighted in subtlety and hidden meanings.

This trait is highly evident in the Gospels. Jesus' listeners were not noticeably interested in whether his parable could be factually authenticated or not. No one ever questioned if the prodigal son or the unjust judge were bona fide people. Rather they were entranced by the underlying meaning of his parables, and doubtless would spend hours discussing the possible interpretations. At least on one occasion the disciples pressed for an outright declaration of the meaning of one particularly elusive parable.

The book of Ruth is an excellent story in point, for not only is it a very fine story (nearly every Biblical commentator declares it the most perfect, artistically speaking, of the Bible's many stories), but it is also very clearly a story and not history. Note the manner in which the book begins: "Long ago, in the time of the judges, there was a famine in the land." This is very much on the order of "Once upon a time."

Another indication that the book of Ruth is essentially a tale is the explanation of certain archaic practices, such as the giving of a sandal as the surety of a spoken agreement. The writer apparently relished these old, forgotten customs, and would tell about them much as someone writing a novel set in Revolutionary War times might interrupt his plot in order to tell about this antiquity or that. And yet, despite all historical pretense, the only certainty in the story of Ruth, historically speaking, is a long-standing tradition that King David had some Moabite blood in his veins.

For all its storyness and literary perfection, the book of

Ruth is primarily the vehicle of a spiritual truth. Goethe felt that Ruth was artistically complete without explanation, but he was wrong. It is more than a lovely tale, and we must not let the beauty of the setting distract our attention from the gem of spiritual truth it holds.

We shall get to that truth later on. It seems best at this point, however, to devote our attention to the story itself.

Rx for a plot

> Thou wast not born for death, immortal Bird!
>   No hungry generations tread thee down;
> The voice I hear this passing night was heard
>   In ancient days by emperor and clown:
> Perhaps the self-same song that found a path
>   Through the sad heart of Ruth, when, sick for home,
>   She stood in tears amid the alien corn . . .
>   "Ode to a Nightingale"   Keats

The story of Ruth begins with the recitation of a series of unbelievably dreadful reverses for a particular family. First driven from their home in Bethlehem by a severe famine, both parents and children became refugees in the land of Moab.

Moab, incidentally, could not have been much of a refuge. Located in the trans-Jordan south and west of Bethlehem, it was a dry, rocky country, fit for little more than the herding of sheep. Moab was something of a famine itself. Life there for this family could not have been much more than a holding operation.

The family did not prosper in Moab. Quite the reverse. The head of the household, a man by the name of Elimelech, soon died, leaving his widow Naomi and their two sons Mahlon and Chilion.

The misfortune of Elimelech's death was accompanied by another type of disappointment for the mother. Instead of marrying Israelite women as they were by religious law supposed to do, the two sons took to wife two women from the tribe of Moab.

This must have been a galling turn of events for Naomi. Such couplings were viewed with roughly the same disapproval which interracial marriage would be looked on today by an entrenched conservative. All sorts of prohibitions were ranged against this practice in those days, as reflected later in the book of Deuteronomy:

> No Ammonite or Moabite, even down to the tenth generation, shall become a member of the assembly of the LORD.
>
> —Deuteronomy 23:3

Naomi may have felt that her cup of bitterness was now full. But soon it would overflow. Her two sons, one after the other, also died, leaving their mother not only with that greatest of all Semitic misfortunes, the lack of an heir and name-bearer, but a pair of pagan daughters-in-law in the bargain.

Clearly, Naomi was one of those characters dear to the heart of every storyteller, the born loser. For Naomi absolutely nothing went right. She was the soap opera heroine for whom everything turned up nettles. She epitomized Murphy's Law: "If anything can go wrong, it will." Misfortune dogged her footsteps. Reverses waited for her around corners. Disasters went before her, and calamities followed.

For poor Naomi there was no recourse after her sons' deaths but to gather up her few possessions and return to Bethlehem in defeat and disgrace, there to throw herself upon the charity of her kinsmen. Thus her array of disasters was crowned with the prospect of that worst of humiliations, destitution.

As she began her journey homeward, it became evident
to her that the daughters-in-law, Orpah and Ruth, were
planning to go along. Naomi pleaded with them to stay with
their own people. She argued that only in Moab would they
have any chance at all to find new husbands and a new life.

In the end, Orpah reluctantly agreed to this advice. But
the other, Ruth, refused to leave Naomi, and did so with a
degree of affection for her mother-in-law which can only be
described as incredible. It was on this occasion that those
matchless words of devotion and loyalty were uttered:
". . . whither thou goest, I will go; and where thou lodgest,
I will lodge: thy people shall be my people, and thy God
my God" (Ruth 1:16).

Together these two forlorn women, partners in misery,
trekked over the outbacks of Moab toward Bethlehem. Perhaps they skirted the eastern and northern shores of the
great Dead Sea, trudging across salt flats, clambering among
the wadis, climbing hillocks—always in danger of exposure
or attack—until at last they crossed the Jordan River and
found themselves in a somewhat friendlier climate.

When they reached Bethlehem, the members of the clan,
astonished by her altered appearance, clustered about Naomi
and listened to her tale of woe. Her feelings of bitterness
were so great that she vented her ire upon God himself.
Like nearly everyone who has ever suffered a grievous series
of reversals, she imagined that God had used her badly, or
even abandoned her, and she did not hesitate to express her
deeply felt resentment. "I went away full, and the LORD has
brought me back empty." Afterwards, with Ruth she settled
down to a life of penury and regret.

But then, when all seemed so hopeless, a rather remarkable thing happened. Ruth, who had gone out to glean the
grain fields—that is, to gather whatever few stalks were left
behind by the reapers—caught the eye of the field's owner, a
wealthy farmer by the name of Boaz. By coincidence, Boaz

also happened to be a close relative of Naomi's dead husband, possibly a first or second cousin.

In a remarkably graphic picture of ancient farm life—the men cutting the grain, and the women gathering it into sheaves—Boaz is encountered talking to his foreman, asking who that pretty, industrious young gleaner out there might be.

Informed of her identity, Boaz immediately went out to her and offered his protection. He told Ruth that she was to keep to his fields and close to his own girls so that she would not be molested, apparently a grim likelihood for any unattached young woman of that day.

One may wonder if they spoke the same language or dialect. A minor point, perhaps, except for the incidental fact that a bit of an accent does sound utterly charming in the ears of a man so obviously infatuated as Boaz. He was enchanted by this mysterious young foreigner, and could hardly wait to ask her to lunch.

So she sat beside the reapers, and he passed her some roasted grain. She ate all she wanted and still had some left over. When she got up to glean, Boaz gave the men orders. "She," he said, "may glean even among the sheaves; do not scold her. Or you may even pull out some corn from the bundles and leave it for her to glean, without reproving her.

—Ruth 2:14–16

The major problem with this intriguing turn of events was that Boaz and Ruth were quite unsuited for one another. They were poles apart. Theirs was a match for which any marriage counselor would have predicted disaster. After all, he was rich and she was poor. He was an Israelite, she a Moabite. He was a person of some standing in the community, while she was practically an outcast.

Yet, as almost everyone must surely realize, any proper love story requires polarity. There is little fascinating about two similar people falling in love. If there is going to be anything to whet interest in a love story, then the man and woman must be utterly different—in rank, in station, in means, in inclination, in temperament, in background. The greater the difference, the more exciting the plot.

Some may argue that in real life such a diversity between a young man and a young woman does not auger well for the future. We must agree. It certainly does not. Similarity is the major desideratum for real-life couples who contemplate matrimony. It is what a man and a woman have in common by way of interests and background which indicates the future success of a proposed marriage.

But this is not true of a story. Here the differences between the hero and the heroine form a vital part of the action, for the hope of every hearer is that these differences will be resolved into a perfect union.

For this reason, young people should be advised that the typical love story should never be viewed as exemplary, but only as a kind of illumination about the power of love. The purpose of emphasizing the differences between lovers in a story is to point up the essential isolation which exists between any given person and another, and the capacity of love to bridge that gap.

More pointedly, in a love story these differences serve to illuminate the mystery of human sexuality itself, and the ability of heterosexual love to overcome the radical psychological and physiological differences between a man and a woman—nay, even more, to indicate the power of love to utilize these very differences in the creation of an even more profound human unity.

To return to the love story at hand, that evening Ruth went to the hovel where she and Naomi now lived. She brought along her windfall of grain, and with wide-eyed wonder told of the kindness of Boaz.

Naomi listened. Carefully. Very likely there was a world-

weary smile on her lips. Cagily she advised Ruth to stick
close to Boaz.

OMNIA VINCIT AMOR

Love is lord of all: yield we, too, to Love!

—Virgil

So the days passed, and soon the time of reaping was
replaced with that of threshing. By now Naomi, who had
been contemplating the attentions of Boaz toward Ruth, had
concocted a plan. The substance of that plan, though neither
Biblical commentator nor expositor seems willing to face the
fact, was seduction. Seduction simple, if not so pure. And
when the time came to put that plan into action, Ruth
acceded with a kind of dovelike innocence.

We cannot blind ourselves to the clear implications of this
section of the story of Ruth, nor allow ourselves to be more
prudish than the Bible itself. According to Naomi's scheme,
Ruth was to make herself as alluring as possible, then late
at night to creep in among the threshers who, fatigued,
well-fed and wined, would be sleeping very soundly. She
would pass among them until she found Boaz, then lie down
and let him make the next and, in Naomi's mind at any
rate, inevitable move.

If Naomi's plan sounds shocking to the modern reader, he
should also be aware of certain mitigating factors.

First, Naomi in part relied upon a tradition known as
levirate marriage, by which a widow could ask a brother-in-
law to father a child, so as to perpetuate the dead man's
name and line.

When brothers live together and one of them dies without
leaving a son, his widow shall not marry outside the family.

Her husband's brother shall have intercourse with her; he shall
take her in marriage and do his duty by her as her husband's
brother. The first son she bears shall perpetuate the dead
brother's name so that it may not be blotted out from Israel.

—Deuteronomy 25:5–6

To be sure, Naomi was tinkering with that tradition to the
point of outright rationalization, for Boaz was only a kinsman
of her husband's family, not a brother. Further, it seems to
have been Elimelech's name, and not that of Mahlon, Ruth's
husband, which Naomi wanted to have perpetuated, though
this distinction may be a quibble.

Yet another softening factor by which Naomi's actions
must be judged was her evident concern for the future of
Ruth. That Naomi herself did not go out to glean the fields
indicates that she might have been quite old by this time, or
ill, and therefore could not help but wonder what would
happen to her beloved daughter-in-law should she die. Perhaps, she reasoned, if a rich man like Boaz were to father a
child by Ruth, surely he would provide continuing care for
the mother at least until the child attained maturity. He
might even make her something of a permanent concubine
within his household.

The most poignant element of mitigation, however, was
the fact of their poverty. Here were two women who lived
on the very borders of starvation. How long or far would
Ruth's gleanings take them? What could be expected during
the dry season to follow? Or in the event of another famine
or plague?

Poverty tends to drive people to acts which they would
otherwise never consider for a moment. A man of perfect
manners can turn into a common thief if faced with starvation
—his own, or that of his family. Men have sold themselves
into slavery, women into prostitution, when faced with the
prospect of destitution.

And who is to blame them? Who can fault Naomi's frantic scheme to find some small element of security for herself and her daughter-in-law, considering the fact that both were unmarriageable, one because of age, and the other because of nationality?

The truth is that this story moves with perfect candor into the abyss of despair, a despair brought about by destitution, and symbolized by Naomi's willingness to let Ruth play the harlot. It is not a pretty picture, but poverty is not a pretty situation, much as we who are affluent are prone to sentimentalize it. Poverty is a degrading state of affairs, and it prompts people to acts of degradation.

It is at this point of the story, then, that the dramatic focus shifts from Naomi and Ruth to Boaz. What counts now is the response of Boaz to the pathetic plottings of two helpless women. It is this which will bring either one more tragedy into Naomi's life, or some well-deserved fortune.

The most tender—almost to the point of incredibility—part of the story is the way in which Boaz treated Ruth's awkward advances as one more token of her loyalty to her mother-in-law. He was neither aroused by the presence of Ruth, nor shocked. Rather he saw into the very heart of her maneuver. Ruth, he realized, was ready to sacrifice herself in any way on Naomi's behalf.

In what must have been some very close whispers, Boaz accepted Ruth's lame explanation about the prerogatives of levirate marriage. He then surprised her by saying that he had been making some investigations along these lines himself. The privilege of any such marriage to her, he explained, was tied to a poor parcel of ground which belonged to Elimelech's estate, and there was a nearer kinsman than himself who was entitled to both.

Boaz went on to say that he was willing to attempt to secure these rights for himself, but this could only be done in an honorable way and in accordance with the Law of Israel. He promised not to delay his efforts in the matter, then bade Ruth to keep still and get some sleep.

Early the next morning, before the threshers were astir, Boaz preserved Ruth's honor by sending her away into the predawn darkness.

In all of his actions, Boaz showed himself not only a person of unusual sensitivity and virtue, but also one who idealized the Mosaic Law to an unusual degree. Here was a man who had been given the perfect opportunity to give in to his natural inclinations. The woman was attractive. She was a foreigner, hence outside the usual moral strictures. The conditions were ideal. Most likely no one would have ever known about the assignation or, if so, would have hardly blamed him.

Yet Boaz refused to treat Ruth as an object for his sexual gratification. He checked his impulses because he cared for Ruth—and that really is what love is all about: care, concern for the other person.

Christians err when they regard the laws of the Old Testament as having an essentially negative character. The greater part of them were as concerned as St. Paul in his epistle to the Galatians, to provoke people to an active pursuit of the good. Boaz exemplified this particular thrust to the Law. He was the embodiment of the man who fulfilled the Law by his positive goodness, and certainly not by merely observing a long list of religious taboos.

Observe, for example, how completely Boaz carried out this admonition to charity from the book of Deuteronomy:

When you reap the harvest in your field and forget a swathe, do not go back to pick it up; it shall be left for the alien, the orphan, and the widow, in order that the LORD your God may bless you in all that you undertake.

—Deuteronomy 24:19

With Ruth returning to report to Naomi, with Boaz left to contemplate the necessary actions of the coming day, the story begins to move toward its perfect conclusion.

Yet, like any good love story, there remained the one, last, seemingly most impassable barrier of all to a happy ending—in this case, the claim of the nearer kinsman. He, not Boaz, had the incontestable right to purchase that mysterious plot of land which yet remained in the estate of Elimelech. Were he to do so, he would assume thereby the right of levirate marriage to Ruth.

We have not been given the name, nor a description of the nearer kinsman in the book of Ruth. Nevertheless we can easily suppose that in at least some versions of its narrated forms he was described as a toothless, bald, fat old lecher, a perfectly ghastly specimen of Hebrew manhood, an absolute shlemiel, and just the wrong person for poor Ruth.

We read that the final, suspense-filled scene took place at the city gate. Early the next morning Boaz went there to wait for the nearer kinsman. When he saw him coming, he called to him, then assembled the required ten elders to witness the business being conducted and whatever agreement might ensue.

In effect, Boaz said to his next-of-kin: "As you know, Elimelech's widow, Naomi, has returned from Moab. I understand that now she wants to sell that little, scrubby piece of land which belonged to him. As nearest kinsman you have the right to buy it, for does not the Law say, 'When one of you is reduced to poverty and sells part of his patrimony, his next-of-kin who has the duty of redemption shall come and redeem what his kinsman has sold'?"

"That is what the Torah says," replied the nearer kinsman.

"Now," Boaz said, swallowing hard and preparing to deliver the fateful question, "are you willing to act as next-of-kin in this matter? For if you are not, then I will do so as next in line and buy the property."

You may be sure that as the story was originally told,
whether in a tent, or around a campfire, or on a long,
drowsy camel ride, the deliberations of the nearer kinsman
were long and drawn out. In his mind he slowly weighed
the pros and cons of the matter. He mentally added up his
own resources. In his imagination he went over Elimelech's
small parcel of ground inch by inch.

"It isn't much," he told himself. "Rocky. Very rocky. And
out of the way. *Way* out of the way. Besides, there's no
water around. I probably couldn't grow cactus there. And I
don't *have* to buy! Boaz here has given me a perfect out.
But still—"

Then, horrors! The nearer kinsman said yes, he would
redeem the property.

Boaz, then, had failed. His hopes had been dashed to
pieces by the very Law which he had so earnestly sought to
uphold. His intention to act honorably had earned him nothing. Ruth would go to the nearer kinsman.

But wait! There remained one small, ever-so-slight hope!
It was the chance that the nearer kinsman did not realize
what the redemption of Elimelech's property entailed—that
Ruth was a part of the package.

But surely he *did* know! Bethlehem was a small place.
This sort of information was readily available.

And yet, perhaps the nearer kinsman was not as bright
as he might be. Possibly he had overlooked this aspect of the
affair. Maybe he had known it once, but later it had slipped
his mind.

But no! No chance! No way! He could not have failed
to realize all that was involved. No point in asking. And
yet . . . And yet . . . For Ruth's sake?

"On the day when you acquire the field from Naomi, you
also acquire Ruth the Moabitess, the dead man's wife, so as
to perpetuate the name of the dead man with his patrimony."

—Ruth 4:5

"The Moabitess? Is that so?" we can imagine the next-of-kin saying, indicating that he was not aware of this aspect of the agreement.

"Well?" said Boaz, looking at the ground, afraid to entertain so much as the slightest hope. "Does that have any bearing on your decision?"

Again a long, interminable silence while all the factors were balanced in that slow, thick mind.

Then miracle of miracles! A *refusal!*

Boaz could hardly believe his ears! Had he heard right? Indeed he had! Already the next-of-kin was explaining to the ten elders that he had patrimony problems of his own, and there was no sense in adding to them. In short, he would have to abandon his prior agreement. Elimelech's property, as well as Ruth, would have to go to Boaz after all.

It would be hard to improve on the story's conclusion as written in the pages of the book of Ruth.

Now in those old days, when property was redeemed or exchanged, it was the custom for a man to pull off his sandal and give it to the other party. This was the form of attestation in Israel. So the next-of-kin said to Boaz, "Acquire it for yourself," and pulled off his sandal. Then Boaz declared to the elders and all the people, "You are witnesses today that I have acquired from Naomi all that belonged to Elimelech and all that belonged to Mahlon and Chilion; and, further, that I have myself acquired Ruth the Moabitess, wife of Mahlon, to be my wife, to perpetuate the name of the deceasd with his patrimony, so that his name may not be missing among his kindred and at the gate of his native place. You are witnesses this day." Then the elders and all who were at the gate said, "We are witnesses. May the LORD make this woman, who has come to your home, like Rachel and Leah, the two who built up the house of Israel. . . ."

So Boaz took Ruth and made her his wife. When they came together, the LORD caused her to conceive and she bore

Boaz a son. Then the women said to Naomi, "Blessed be the
LORD today, for he has not left you without a next-of-kin. May
the dead man's name be kept alive in Israel. The child will
give you new life and cherish you in your old age; for your
daughter-in-law who loves you, who has proved better to you
than seven sons, has borne him." Naomi took the child and
laid him in her lap and became his nurse. Her neighbours
gave him a name: "Naomi has a son," they said; "we will call
him Obed." He was the father of Jesse, the father of David.

—Ruth 4:7–11, 13–17

Boaz and his Ruth thus lived happily ever after in the
company of Naomi and that promising little heir, Obed. But
beyond the happiness which is due all young lovers lay the
significant fact that the storyteller accorded to this couple
that most desirable of honors among the people of God—a
prominent part in the ancestry of David.

And so it came about that Ruth, the destitute young
Moabite widow, became great-grandmother to a king.

THE REAL MEANING OF THIS STORY

In Christ there is no East or West,
In him no South or North,
But one great fellowship of love
Throughout the whole wide earth.

—John Oxenham

The meaning of the story of Ruth becomes clear when it
is contrasted against the somber soil in which it rooted and
took flower.

Some four or five centuries before the birth of Christ, a
few of the Judean survivors of the Babylonian Captivity had
begun to trickle back down into the Holy Land. They found

their beloved Judah a shambles. Jerusalem was a charred ruin, its walls leveled to the ground, its Temple a pile of rubble.

The few Judeans who had remained behind at the time of the Captivity had allowed both religion and culture to degenerate into a terrible state. Further, there were many strange people about—Edomites, Ammonites, Moabites, people with strange languages and habits, people who had come in as squatters to occupy the abandoned properties of Judah.

Worst of all, as far as the returnees were concerned, was the widespread practice of intermarriage between these foreigners and native Judeans. To those who had so carefully preserved their religious heritage in far-off Babylon despite prejudice and persecution, these casual alliances seemed like the worst apostasy imaginable.

The reaction to this state of affairs was almost predictable. The returning exiles, many of whom were of a priestly caste, men who had for years dreamed of their return to a bright new kingdom and covenant, vigorously set about the restoration of a purified religion.

The word "puritan" would be quite applicable to the next few generations of Israel's history. The leaders became obsessed with religious and racial purity. They grew extremely legalistic. The old religious rules were dusted off and followed with a vengeance. Doctrine became exact. Latitude was regarded as heresy. Worship turned joyless and rigorous.

This movement reached its peak, as we have already seen, around the time of Nehemiah and Ezra (approximately 450–400 B.C.).

One of the more heartless excesses in this period of religious zeal was the encouragement of Jewish men to divorce their foreign-born wives. From all that can be gathered, it mattered not whether these women conformed to the religion of their husbands or not. If they were not of Judean

ancestry, they were simply cut loose from husbands and
homes and left to fend for themselves.

> When all this had been done, some of the leaders approached
> me and said, "The people of Israel, including priests and Levites,
> have not kept themselves apart from the foreign population and
> from the abominable practices of the Canaanites, the Hittites, the
> Perizzites, the Jebusites, the Ammonites, the Moabites, the
> Egyptians, and the Amorites. They have taken women of these
> nations as wives for themselves and their sons, so that the holy
> race has become mixed with the foreign population; and the
> leaders and magistrates have been the chief offenders." When I
> heard this news, I rent my robe and mantle, and tore my hair
> and my beard. . . .
>
> While Ezra was praying and making confession, prostrate
> in tears before the house of God, a very great crowd of
> Israelites assembled round him, men, women, and children, and
> they all wept bitterly. Then Shecaniah son of Jehiel, one of the
> family of Elam, spoke up and said to Ezra, "We have committed
> an offence against our God in marrying foreign wives, daughters
> of the foreign population. But in spite of this, there is still hope
> for Israel. Now, therefore, let us pledge ourselves to our God
> to dismiss all these women and their brood, according to your
> advice, my lord. . . . and they dismissed them, together with
> their children.
>
> —Ezra 9:1–3, 10:1–3, 44

No one can read these compassionless words and fail to
realize afresh that men have done terrible deeds in the name
of religion. T. S. Eliot's *Murder in the Cathedral* suggests
that one of the most insidious temptations which faces men
is to do the right thing for the wrong reason. The opposite
temptation, to do the wrong thing for the right reason, may
not be quite so insidious, but its effects are generally more
disastrous. Deeds of cruelty and violence in the cause of
religious or political ideals have been all too common in the

affairs of men both past and present. Doing what is wrong so as to exalt what is imagined to be right is the venemous tendency of the self-righteous, and the succumbing to it has accounted for some of the sorriest chapters in human history.

Against such an onslaught of fanaticism the book of Ruth —and also, incidentally, the book of Jonah—came to take a stand. Based upon the likelihood that Moabite blood ran in King David's veins, the story of Ruth brought its winsome plea for tolerance and charitableness among men.

But there is much more to Ruth than a simple humanitarianism. Much deeper lies an insight into the ways of God with men, an insight which proclaims that God is not bound by human institutions. The book of Ruth tells us that God does not, and will not, allow himself to be imprisoned by walls of any kind, be they theological, or ecclesiastical, nationalistic or racial. Ruth stands opposed to any notion of "holy race" by offering the gentle reminder that the things which bind men together are far more important than the things which separate them.

The understanding that God was equally at work outside the borders of Israel was a latecomer to that nation's religion. Not until the prophets of the eighth and seventh centuries B.C. was there any genuine criticism of the prevailing doctrines of religious exclusivism. In Ruth the message of God's universality in his dealings with men was given a very persuasive and artistic treatment.

Yet it remained for the New Testament to bring this rather radical idea to fulfillment. The seeds of Ruth bore fruit in the parable of the Good Samaritan; in Christ's assurance that "Many, I tell you, will come from east and west to feast with Abraham, Isaac, and Jacob in the Kingdom of heaven"; in the Fourth Gospel's mighty declaration that God so loved the world—*all* of it, not just some special part—that he gave his only begotten Son; in the Apostle

Paul's determination to preach among the Gentiles without superimposing upon them the constricting ceremonial requirements of circumcision and dietary laws; in Peter's sudden and splendid realization that "God has no favourites."

The book of Ruth, then. Not only a perfect story; but a perfect moral too!

IX JUDAS:
VARIATIONS ON AN ENIGMA

If he had been as you and you as he
You would have slipt like him. . . .
                    —Measure for Measure

There can be little doubt that the contemporary student of the Bible has a far more accurate understanding of the events and setting of the night before the Crucifixion than his counterpart of the second century, or any other century for that matter.

The New Testament accounts of the first Maundy Thursday, together with clues provided by historical and archaeological investigation, can be made to fit together like a jigsaw puzzle with only a few of the pieces missing.

The picture is nearly complete. We know how Jerusalem looked some 1,942 years ago. With considerable precision the location of the places involved in that tragic event can be pinpointed: the upper room, Gethsemane, the palaces of Caiaphas and Herod, the Antonia Tower. Scholars can make likely surmises about the routes taken by the Nazarene as he was accompanied during the earlier part of the evening by his closest friends, and later by his bitterest enemies.

The timetable of events can also be closely plotted. In his

book *The Day Christ Died,* Jim Bishop presents a detailed chronology of the Passion. Based on thorough research, his calculations cannot be far wrong.

We can even be reasonably certain about the weather conditions that evening. The moon, a shade past full, illuminated the landscape with its pallid brightness. The warm southeast wind tapered off toward nightfall, dropping the temperature into the fifties. There were no clouds.

This paragraph is based on a number of surmises. Beginning with the assumption that the evening in question was that of April sixth or seventh (Nisan 13–14 or 14–15), A.D. 30, it goes on to suppose that the full moon was calculated on the ripe side, since the first day of the lunar month depended upon the visual sighting of the "sickle" of the new moon. This would make the midmonth moon a shade past full.

As to the remaining meteorological assumptions, one could speculate that the willingness of Jesus and his disciples to spend the night in the open suggests the presence of a sirocco or "khamsin wind." This dry desert wind was common to April, tending to alternate with the "latter rains." Had there been this rain, together with its dank, cold westerly wind, Jesus and his followers would doubtless have remained in a sheltered place.

The persons who took part in this momentous drama also tend to manifest themselves with some clarity. At the center is Jesus of Nazareth. While the state of his mind will ever remain a profound mystery, his followers made subsequent attempts to describe what they remembered of him that night. Their reminiscences became woven into the Biblical account of Jesus' agonized prayer in Gethsemane.

Others more clearly reveal their deeply human response to the crisis of this most memorable evening in history. One can discern the wily ploys of Caiaphas, the jaded fascination of Herod Antipas, the indecision of the weak and unpopular

Roman procurator, Pontius Pilate. Even the soldiers, with their coarse, cruel humor, come through.

Among the disciples, Simon Peter stands in the foreground. We see him clearly: at first blustering and reckless in Gethsemane, then, as he tries to warm himself in the courtyard of the high priest's palace, whining cowardly denials of all acquaintance with Jesus. As for Peter's ten remaining companions, their initial confusion at the moment of Jesus' arrest, followed by panic-ridden rout, seems a plausible reaction even from the perspective of nearly two thousand years.

One figure, however, continues an enigma. Toward the center of the puzzle we find a large and frustrating blank. The surrounding pieces suggest that this one is dark and demonic. Yet we cannot be sure. For what can be said of Judas Iscariot? Does that absent piece turn up a villain, as most people assume? Or is there something else to be said of the man who was Jesus' disciple and friend for many years, but who for some unfathomable reason turned betrayer at the end?

Little is known of Judas Iscariot. Doubtless his act of betrayal erased all brighter memories that might have been held of him. In the Scriptures he is always listed as a turncoat. Only one oblique reference to his career as a disciple may be found in the Bible. It is said that when a woman honored Jesus by pouring an expensive oil upon his head (an act of deepest reverence in those times), Judas questioned if the cost of the oil might not have been better used as a donation to the poor. It is possible that behind the writer's prejudice—he says that in this instance Judas was motivated by personal greed—we might catch a glimpse of a very high-minded person. Also, it must be added, there might be evidence here of a certain spirit of independence.

Most scholars believe that his surname Iscariot derives from the Judean village of Kerioth. If so, Judas was probably the lone Judean among the Twelve.

How he encountered Jesus or what compelled him to become a follower is not known. Evidently a high zeal was at work, for not only was he able to gain a place among an exclusively Galilean group, but he took a position of considerable responsibility, that of treasurer. Whether or not he was a thief, as one of the Gospel writers insists, must be accepted with some hesitancy. It must be remembered that this would be an ex post facto judgment. Also, the particular purse in question could never have been full enough to warrant the attention of a compulsive filcher.

Nevertheless, Judas did betray Jesus. His act of treachery was performed sometime during that last fateful week. Arrangements were made for the arrest of Jesus at a time when he would not be surrounded by his many admirers. But what the terms of this agreement were, and with whom they were made, is not entirely clear. Apparently money changed hands.

Any compassionate assessment of Judas must take into account the extent of his perfidy. The most that Judas actually did was to reveal the whereabouts of Jesus, and, in the pale uncertain moonlight, to distinguish his master from the others. The kiss of betrayal seems heinous beyond description. Yet it must be allowed that we have no evidence that Judas further testified against Jesus.

Indeed, those moments in the Garden seem to have been followed immediately by intense remorse on Judas' part. According to one account, Judas attempted to repurchase the freedom of Jesus. His failure at this, together with the inevitability of Jesus' conviction and execution for the crime of sedition, drove Judas Iscariot to despair and suicide.

THREE ANSWERS TO A RIDDLE

But *why* did Judas betray Jesus? What forces caused a trusted follower to turn traitor?

To ask the question is to precipitate one into the baffling mazes of human behavior. Here easy answers are hard to come by. Most likely Judas himself would have found it impossible to account for his action, except to agree with one of the evangelists that "Satan entered into him." Every person has committed acts which afterward have caused anguished recriminations. "How," runs a refrain familiar to every man, "could I have ever done a thing like that?"

Still, a number of theories about Judas have been proposed over the centuries. Most of them can be summarized under three general categories. That is to say, Judas' betrayal must have stemmed from avarice, disillusionment, or provocation. Each has it points, each its drawbacks.

The most widely held theory assumes that Judas was motivated by avarice. Judas, accordingly, was a thief and a villain who sold his leader for money.

Here one finds the traditional Judas, the Judas recognizable by his cunning, malevolent face in the various paintings of the Twelve.

> He's Judas to a tittle, that man is!
> Just such a face!

Thus Robert Browning's Fra Lippo Lippi insults a man. Tintoretto, in his rendition of the Last Supper, makes Judas left-handed, a characteristic regarded as literally "sinister" (the Latin word *sinister* means "left" or "left-handed") in earlier times.

Such also is the poet Dante's understanding of Judas. In the *Inferno* the betrayer is consigned to the lowest depths of hell.

Some proponents of the avarice theory suggest that Judas began as a good man who was eventually warped by petty pilfering from the disciples' common treasury.

Others maintain that Judas was dishonest from the beginning, merely biding his time until Jesus' gain in popular support would provide him with a financial coup. When this support failed to materialize, so the theory continues, Judas declared bankruptcy and got out with what he could.

On the surface of it, avarice *does* seem to be the most obvious motive behind Judas' betrayal.

But a closer examination reveals this to be in fact the least likely explanation of them all, for it leaves far too many questions unanswered. For example, why were not the disciples earlier aware of Judas' unprincipled avarice? It seems impossible to live in such proximity to a person for three years and not develop some suspicions.

The contrary seems more likely. Judas, an outlander to begin with, had earned the total confidence of his peers. Indeed, so trusted was he that when Jesus announced that one of the disciples would betray him, no one seemed to suspect Judas. His absence during the latter part of the last supper apparently went unquestioned. And surely the disciples would not have fallen asleep in Gethsemane had Judas been regarded as a threat.

Other questions crowd the theory. If so avaricious, why did Judas sell out for such a paltry sum as thirty pieces of silver? If motivated so simply by greed, why did not Judas take his blood money, declare good riddance, and retire to Kerioth? Why the remorse and suicide? Avarice, after all, flourishes only in the absence of conscience; and the frantic attempts of Judas to secure the release of Jesus, together with his suicide, reveals a most sensitive conscience.

A second theory fastens onto the possibility that Judas may have become disillusioned with Jesus. This disillusionment has been given many forms, from a disappointment in the capacity of Jesus to rally sufficient popular support for an anti-Roman rebellion to a bitter division over the Nazarene's criticism of traditional religion.

Some feel that Jesus' triumphal approach to Jerusalem culminating in the cleansing of the Temple may have stirred the ire of Judas. Dorothy Sayers, the English novelist and lay theologian, has offered the interesting suggestion that this series of events in Jesus' life convinced Judas that Jesus had sold out to worldly messianic aspirations. A similar theory holds that only the sudden conviction that Jesus was a false messiah could have driven Judas to so radical a deed.

The disillusionment theory in all of its forms has a rather high degree of plausibility. Disillusionment tends to cause reckless acts. A disillusioned person feels cheated, even betrayed; and betrays in turn.

Still, this theory is open to some cross-examination. First, it hardly seems possible that the thoroughgoing consistency of Jesus' teachings could create the illusion from which disillusionment ensues. One finds nothing in the Gospels to indicate that Jesus wove a spell of illusory hopes.

Moreover, the theory compels one to ask why Judas did not offer testimony against his master. It must be recalled that the accusations against Jesus were based on such flimsy evidence that Pilate became convinced of his innocence. Yet, only a few sworn statements from a turncoat like Judas would have provided Pilate with sufficient proof for any Roman governor of that time. A disillusioned Judas would undoubtedly have been willing to testify. But apparently he never did.

Further, the disillusionment theory cannot sufficiently account for the remorse of Judas after Jesus had been captured. One would expect some bleak satisfaction from a disillusioned Judas, not a frenzied effort to reverse the consequences of his act.

A third, the provocation theory, offers the possibility that Judas' action was an attempt to provoke Jesus into a counteraction. Interestingly, a form of this argument was put forward over one hundred years ago by Thomas De Quincey. The present development of Biblical studies has rendered such an interpretation the most likely of all.

This explanation rests upon the assumption that Judas shared with the other disciples a mistaken notion of the messiahship of Jesus. All assumed that Jesus was appointed by God to lead a popular uprising against the Roman occupiers and reestablish the ancient monarchy of King David. Involved in this conviction was the belief that when the confrontation with Rome came, the forces of heaven would side with the small popular army of the Christ to crush the Roman oppressor.

Despite Jesus' clear teaching to the contrary, the disciples could not seem to rid themselves of this popular messianic notion.

Accordingly, Judas attempted to *provoke* a confrontation between the forces of Rome and the forces of Jesus by delivering Jesus into the hands of his enemies. By so doing, Judas felt that Jesus would be forced to summon his heavenly legions. The "Day of the Lord" would then come to pass, and the enemies of Israel would be vanquished.

Plausible though such an explanation might be, it too bears some questioning. Why, we ask, did Judas act alone if he were motivated along these lines? One would expect that the other disciples would have been brought into such a scheme. Also, why take payment? If such a confrontation were all that Judas desired, he could have arranged it without the bounty.

ON BEHALF OF JUDAS

Clearly, no single theory explaining the perfidy of Judas will ever be found. And yet all of them together can undo the commonly held opinion that the betrayer of Jesus was a totally evil man. He was not that. Rather, he was quite human. He possessed a collection of traits both good and bad. He had his vices. But who would deny that Judas had certain virtues too?

Like all men he held hopes and suffered fears. Religion and irreligion jostled together inside him. He shared the privation of the disciples as well as their bounty. In one tragic moment he failed so utterly that he felt he was beyond mercy itself, and so went and hanged himself.

But one commentator, writing of the pitiable Judas, directs attention to one aspect of the story generally overlooked. Of all the disciples, he notes, Judas was the only one to raise his voice in Jesus' behalf that last day. Peter denied him. All but John vanished. Only the man from Kerioth put in a word for the doomed Nazarene.

"Whatever it was, on the bleak morning of the Crucifixion, the man called Judas stood in the temple court, threw his thirty pieces of silver on the stone floor, and with them his solitary, anguished ballot for the Nazarene. It was too late. The polls were closed."*

* Paul Scherer in *The Interpreter's Bible*, vol. 8, pp. 390 f.

X BARNABAS:
COMPANION OF PAUL

> . . . that best portion of a good man's life
> His little, nameless, unremembered acts
> Of kindness and of love.
>
> —Wordsworth

To a student of the Bible the figure of St. Paul is such a massive and forceful personality, so unique, so powerful and of such consequence in the development of the church's theology, that one is very likely to overlook the great men who were his companions and fellow apostles during those first critical decades of the life of the Christian church.

Barnabas, for example. Who knows very much at all about this compelling individual beyond the fact that he accompanied Paul (or, more accurately, Paul accompanied *him*) on the first missionary journey? Like the author of Acts, we tend to be so intrigued by the doings of Paul that the moment he and Barnabas part over an unfortunate difference of opinion, our attention naturally follows Paul, leaving Barnabas to fade off into oblivion.

And yet if, in this instance, we turn our attention from the large flamboyant canvas that is Paul to the smaller one that is Barnabas, we shall be richly rewarded. For Barnabas

was not only one of the most winsome personalities of the
Bible; he also happened to be one whose intervention on
two critical occasions had an incalculable influence on the
destiny of apostolic Christianity.

Shift your gaze for the moment, then, from that more
imposing and dominant personality of the post-Resurrection
church and, using the materials given us in Acts and certain
of the letters of Paul, examine that lesser-known figure called
Barnabas. We shall not, of course, get very far from Paul in
any event. Paul's influence is pervasive. But we can be
reminded once more that in the Bible, as in life, one often
comes across treasures in dim and unsuspected corners.

THE ADVOCATE OF SAUL

We first come upon Barnabas in the early chapters of
the Acts of the Apostles, where we are told that a person
from Cyprus by the name of Joseph laid the proceeds from
the sale of his property at the feet of the apostles. This
Joseph is described as being a Levite—a man of distinguished
Jewish lineage, one who doubtless had been very active in
the affairs of his home synagogue on the island of Cyprus.

It seems likely that this Joseph was already a member of
the Christian community when he made his offering. Euse-
bius, the fourth-century church historian, suggests that this
man was converted by Jesus himself, that he was one of
the "seventy" mentioned in Luke's Gospel who were sent
out two and two. But if he was not one of these minor
disciples, then at least he was one of the first converts
after Pentecost, since the communal holding of property was
one of the earliest and most short-lived phases in the life of
the church as she began to struggle toward a recognizable
theology and polity.

Joseph of Cyprus was quickly given another name by

the apostles. Perhaps they wanted to distinguish him from another prominent churchman named Joseph Barsabbas. But more likely it was because he was so outstandingly good, so kind, so pleasant to have around. A generous estimate of the traits of others, a deep faith in the essential goodness of human nature and an infectious optimism combined to give this man what must have been a marvelously sunny disposition. We nowhere read that he was a profound thinker or a powerful preacher. But he warmed many a heart in his day. He reminds us of that buoyant Oxford classmate of Dr. Johnson encountered by him after many years on the streets of London. While telling Johnson what had happened during the intervening years, he said, "I have tried too in my time to be a philosopher; but, I don't know how, cheerfulness was always breaking in."

Such was the disposition of Joseph of Cyprus, and because of it the apostles gave him a nickname which had the form of a surname: *Barnabas,* "son of encouragement."

We hear no more of Barnabas after the presentation of his small patrimony to the authorities of the church until his reappearance in Jerusalem with an intense, moody young Pharisee in tow. This strange fellow came from a city far to the north called Tarsus, and he bore the name of Saul. Jerusalem, it might be recalled here, remained the center of the Christian church until the destruction of that city in A.D. 70. Before anyone could be commissioned as a bona fide preacher of the Gospel, he presumably had to be cleared by such chief apostles as James, John and Peter.

We read that the apostles were alarmed at the sight of Barnabas' companion. And justifiably! Saul was known far and wide as one of the most ruthless opponents of those who believed that Jesus was the Christ. Clearly he was not a man to be tampered with. Saul was not the sort who did things in half measures. Quite the contrary. Saul was one of those deadly serious sorts who, when he took up a cause, did so with the fierceness of a dragon. No armchair believer he! Ideas were almost tangible to this compulsive man, and the wrongness or rightness of them made a world of difference. He might switch one set of ideas for another, but Saul was the type who would fight in any event.

The apostles may well have suspected that Saul was an infiltrator. They might have thought him to be an agent of the Roman empire or the Jewish religious establishment who was engaged to spy out this Christianity business, then turn over his findings to the authorities for immediate and thorough liquidation of the enterprise.

But not Barnabas. Barnabas was a trusting soul.

"Ah, there goes Barnabas again," we can almost imagine one of that little band of apostles saying. "Up to his old tricks."

"Yes," another might have added with a grim nod. "Incurably gullible about people, that chap. Tends to take everyone at his word."

But gentle, hopeful Barnabas was as persistent as he was pleasant. He pleaded the cause of this former one-man religious inquisition. He told the reluctant apostles "how on the road he [Saul] had seen the Lord, who spoke to him, and how at Damascus he had preached boldly in the name of Jesus" (Acts 9:27).

And so it was probably through the assurances of Barnabas that Saul of Tarsus was given provisional certification by the authorities in Jerusalem.

What followed this brief appearance of Barnabas and Saul before the council in Jerusalem cannot be easily determined. The author of Acts does not seem to know, nor does Paul in his letter to the Galatians shed much light on the mysterious "fourteen years." It seems safe to conjecture that shortly after Saul's case was presented to the apostles, Barnabas was given responsibility for the church in Antioch. This church was an active one. It was here that the term "Christian"

came into being. A zealous program of evangelization was
being carried on in the area, and it seems reasonable to assume that Barnabas invited Saul to share in this work.

During this period Saul seems to have been something of a
protégé to Barnabas. Perhaps the word "apprentice" is more
suitable. Whichever, the likelihood that Saul served in a
subordinate capacity is buttressed by several facts. First,
there appears in Acts a list of the preachers and catechists
attached to the church in Antioch. It is possible that Luke,
the author of Acts, picked up this list during his travels.
Whatever its origin, it seems an authentic indication of
conditions in Antioch at the time, and the fact is that
Barnabas' name heads the list and Saul's comes last. Second
is the fact that when the first missionary journey was arranged, its primary objective was the evangelization of Cyprus,
the native territory of Barnabas. One is forced to conclude
that the proposal for this missionary journey came from
Barnabas, not Saul.

A MOMENTOUS JOURNEY TO CYPRUS

Barnabas may have had the idea of preaching the Gospel
in Cyprus for some time. We can easily picture him looking
forward to the day when he could bring the good news to
his relatives and friends back home. When, at length, the
church in Antioch was led by the Spirit to support this
mission, Barnabas may have recommended that one of the
most promising preachers around, Saul, be allowed to go
along as a fellow missionary. The suggestion that his young
cousin, John Mark, be taken along also must have come
from Barnabas.

In order to journey to Cyprus from Antioch, the three
had to cross overland to the port of Seleucia, then embark
on a sea journey of some one hundred and twenty-five

miles southwest to the Cyprian port of Salamis. One can almost visualize these men on the deck of that small sailing ship, a ship similar to the present day Arabian dhow—rough planking, pitched seams, leather sails. As they watched the land behind them recede into the distance, each was likely thinking of his destination in a slightly different way. For Barnabas it was home. For John Mark it must have been a place of unimaginable adventure. But for Saul it was a land filled with people "having no hope and without God in the world."

And what would come of it all? Would the message they were bringing across the mysterious, unpredictable sea be accepted? Would the church take root here? Would prayers be answered? Would the hopes of the Antiochene Christians be realized?

Whatever their private thoughts as the journey began, we can be certain that they did not begin to imagine the enormous consequences of this first tentative Christian probe into the regions north and east of the Mediterranean. Saul, surely, never dreamed that he would return to Antioch with a new name and a new mission. Nor did John Mark suspect that he would leave his two companions before the journey was over. Nor did Barnabas realize that the person who stood silently beside him looking out across the water would soon be more the master than the apprentice, that Saul of Tarsus was about to find himself, was on his way to becoming the dominant evangelist and theologian of the apostolic church.

The consequences of their journey would be momentous. But as the three of them watched the uneasy Mediterranean spreading gray and sullen toward the western sky, they were surely unaware of what lay ahead.

Barnabas, Saul and John Mark landed at Salamis on the western tip of Cyprus and gradually made their way across the island to the city of Paphos at the other end. We

can surmise that their missionary strategy at this time was
pretty much as follows. They would visit the small Jewish
enclaves here and there in the predominantly Gentile culture,
making personal contacts and engaging in personal witness.
On the sabbath they would attend the local synagogue.
As learned guests they would be asked to comment on the
Scriptures which were read as a part of the service. Then
either Saul or Barnabas would express his conviction that
these Scriptures had been fulfilled in the life, death and
resurrection of one Jesus of Nazareth. This man, they would
say, was the long awaited Messiah, the Christ. He was the
one of whom the Torah and the prophets spoke. It was all
there, they said, in the scrolls.

This missionary strategy was effective, all right. But there
was one drawback. It tended to be restricted to Jews and
Jewish proselytes.

Great movements in history have often begun in quite
unprepossessing ways. Take, for instance, the feet of Rosa
Parks. Mrs. Parks was riding home from work on a bus in
Montgomery, Alabama, back in the year 1955. Her feet were
very tired, so when the bus driver told Mrs. Parks, a black
woman, to move to the rear as more and more white cus-
tomers boarded, the condition of her feet prompted her to
refuse.

Mrs. Parks was arrested. What followed is history: the
Montgomery bus boycott, the emergence of Martin Luther
King, the great moral and legal struggle against the en-
trenched forces of racism in this country.

In a similar way, it is quite probable that a chance encounter between the three Antiochene missionaries and a
minor Roman official by the name of Sergius Paulus provided
the beginning of a movement of stupendous consequences,
one whose repercussions have lasted for nearly two thousand
years and show no signs of ending. I refer to the transforma-

tion of Christianity from a primarily Jewish religion into a primarily Gentile one.

At the time of this meeting, Sergius Paulus was under the influence of a religious quack named Bar-Jesus. Described as an intelligent man, Paulus seemed able to distinguish true religion from false, and quickly became converted to the teachings of Barnabas and Saul.

Can we hazard the speculation that this conversion may have had as great an influence on Saul as on Sergius Paulus? I believe we can, especially when we realize that it is quite likely that Saul renamed himself Paul because of this man. There seems no other adequate explanation for the change. The name Paul, after all, is not descriptive in the sense that Barnabas is. Paul means, simply, "little." And while Saul of Tarsus may have been short of stature, he was not little in any other way.

The more likely explanation is that on the occasion of the conversion of Sergius Paulus, Saul realized for the first time his unique ability to communicate with Gentiles. And, he may have reasoned, if God had in mind that he should preach to the Gentiles, then he ought to do so with a Gentile name. It was a case of being all things to all men. Hitherto he had been Saul to the Jews; from now on he would be Paul to the Gentiles. His encounter with a Roman civil servant persuaded him that the Sergius Pauluses of the world needed a Paul who would bring them the story of Jesus Christ.

Paul's convictions about evangelizing Gentiles must have developed very quickly. In all probability there had been no original intention of extending this missionary journey beyond the borders of Cyprus. But now Paul had the bit in his mouth. He had a new idea—an apostolate to non-Jews. And he wanted to try it out before returning to Antioch. It seems likely that he persuaded Barnabas to

accompany him to the mainland to the north, an area today
that is a part of Turkey.

For some reason which cannot be fully explained, John
Mark decided that rather than continue on, he would turn
back. In describing Mark's defection, Luke, the author of
Acts, gives us a puzzling phrase. He writes that John Mark
returned not to Antioch, but to Jerusalem. The words—
their implications—are most curious. Was this a slip of the
pen? Or was John Mark a resident of Jerusalem and not
Antioch? Or does one find lurking here the possibility that
Mark had become convinced that Paul was overstepping
certain bounds in this matter of evangelizing the Gentiles,
and he wanted to check it out with the "pillars" in Jerusalem?

Whatever the reason, Mark's sudden departure rankled
Paul. The incident would have unfortunate consequences for
all three later on.

THE ODD COUPLE

Paul and Barnabas sailed on by themselves to the city of
Perga. From this seaport city they made their way inland to
the surrounding regions. Here for the first time their teaching
in the synagogues met with active resistance. One wonders
why. Had Paul begun to sharpen the distinction between
Christian and Jew? Our information is too sketchy to tell,
but the possibility is certainly there. We do know that at
this time the violent rejection of the Gospel by the Jews
caused Paul to announce that in the future he would deal
directly with the Gentiles.

And Paul and Barnabas spoke out boldly (to the Jews) saying,
"It was necessary that the word of God should be spoken first
to you. Since you thrust it from you, and judge yourself unworthy of eternal life, behold, we turn to the Gentiles."

—Acts 13:46

The consequences of this decision were far greater than most people might assume. The reverberations continue to this day. We shall deal shortly with one of the first issues to become involved. But let it suffice at this point to be reminded that, for the earliest believers, to be a Christian was in essence to be a certain kind of Jew—one who followed the Mosaic Law, was circumcised, worshiped in the synagogue, and was identified by birth or conversion with the religion of Israel. Christianity was an addition to, not a replacement of, Judaism. It meant that besides being a devout Jew, one possessed the additional conviction that the promised Messiah and Lord had now come in the person of Jesus of Nazareth, a conviction which was sealed through the rite of baptism and nourished by participation in the anticipatory supper.

Paul's decision, therefore, to preach Christ directly to the Gentiles and to do so outside the context of Judaism was nothing less than an incredible radicalism which must have strained even the accommodating personality of Barnabas. No one had been prepared for such an application of the Gospel as this. It was more than a novelty. It was a theological revolution.

Incidentally, while they were in the Lycaonian city of Lystra, there occurred an off-beat happening which provides us with what might be described as a blurred photograph of Paul and Barnabas. It followed Paul's healing of a congenital cripple. The deed so astonished the inhabitants of that city that they deluded themselves into imagining that a delegation from their pantheon of gods had paid them a visit. Paul they supposed to be Hermes, while Barnabas was regarded as the incarnation of Zeus.

The distinction suggests, among other things, that Barnabas was regarded as the leader of the two. Hermes, after all, was an inferior Greek deity. No one gave much thought to Hermes. He was no more than one of those minor gods who carried messages around on behalf of his betters. That and being one of the lesser sons of Zeus were the only distinctions that a Hermes could boast.

But Zeus was one of the most prominent of Greek deities. Zeus, like his Roman counterpart Jupiter, was the god of the sky. Zeus was the god whose voice was heard in the thunder. Zeus was the name given to the supreme power by such intellectuals as Plato and Aeschylus.

The identification of Barnabas with Zeus suggests more than his assumed authority over Paul. If one starts with the artistic renderings of Zeus in those days, adds to it the psychological principle that large muscular men tend to be so self-secure that they are naturally inclined to be easygoing, one arrives at a rather graphic depiction of Barnabas as he must have appeared to his contemporaries. He would have been a large man, a man who towered over the diminutive Paul.

Beyond this, one's imagination must take over. This author sees him as having a massive head, a broad pleasant face, a princely Hebrew nose and a full Levitical beard. For some reason I would like to think that Barnabas was gap-toothed, possibly on the principle that people with spaces between their teeth have a way of turning out to be the pleasantest of folk. I would give him a thick neck, the chest of a blacksmith and the girth of an innkeeper. His hands were like hams, though as a good Jew he would not have liked the simile. Over-all, he was of such bulk that men were disinclined to trifle with him; so it comes as no surprise that while we learn that Paul was stoned on this first missionary journey, there is no record of this happening to Barnabas.

It might be useful here to expand this word picture so as to include Paul. For they were an odd couple, these two. As different as two people can possibly be, and yet united by a common cause greater than the both of them. If

Barnabas was a great bear of a man who had a deep, rich love for his fellow man, then what kind of person was Paul?

Paul was quite opposite to Barnabas, both in physical appearance and temperament. He was a man who bore the aggressiveness of the small and sickly, for he was both. In II Corinthians he acknowledged the personal slight of his theological opponents that "his bodily presence is weak." A document from the following century would record that Paul was short, bald and bowlegged.

Within this small disfigured body burned a strange personality. Since we are comparing Paul with Barnabas, we must admit that he bore little of the cordiality of his mentor. Paul was not a warm person. Indeed, he was something of a fanatic. Paul was one of that thin-lipped, humorless and more than somewhat obsessive band of Christian dogmatists like Calvin, Loyola, Edwards and Athanasius—the last of whom was known as the "hammer of heretics"—in whose veins run the ice water of dogmatic truth. These are the type whom the little girl must have had in mind when she prayed, "O God, make all the bad people good, and the good people nice."

One must admire the breed, must admit its necessity, even. But one would much prefer inviting someone like Barnabas to dinner! It is almost ludicrous to imagine the four mentioned above at meat together. One pictures them nibbling abstemiously, and all the while snarling at each other over theological niceties.

To expand the idea a bit further, one does not hear the sound of birds and children in the writings of Paul. He passed through some of the most spectacular scenery in the world during his travels, yet never mentions it. If he alludes to the pleasures of life, it is always from the negative side. His self-discipline was vigorous. He "buffeted," which is to say whipped, his body so that it would not interfere with his immense tasks and cares.

That these two diverse personalities were able to tolerate each other at all is in itself a witness to the power of the message they jointly bore. After Cyprus their partnership would come under great strain. Paul would rise far above Barnabas, his onetime teacher, on the wings of a theological issue which Barnabas probably never fully understood. Yet Barnabas supported Paul on this issue, and very likely once again in the face of a contrary majority.

There is no indication of malice or jealousy on the part of Barnabas as he watched Paul soar into prominence. And when the break came, it was due to the magnanimity of Barnabas and not any difference of opinion between them over this first great theological test for the church, a matter to which we now turn our attention.

THE QUESTION OF GENTILE CONVERTS

At length this first and critical missionary journey drew to a close. Barnabas and Paul reembarked for home and after many days at sea arrived back in Antioch.

The welcome for the two of them can only be imagined. Paul and Barnabas must have spent many hours telling and retelling of their triumphs and defeats, their hardships and rewards, during which "God . . . opened a door of faith to the Gentiles."

There can be no doubt, however, that Paul's new emphasis on direct evangelism among the Gentiles must have stirred certain apprehensions within this community of Jewish and proselyte Christians at Antioch. What did he mean by all this? Was he really suggesting that a man could be a follower of Christ without being under the discipline of the Mosaic Law? Was this door of faith of which Saul of Tarsus spoke some sort of illicit back door? And why had he taken to calling himself by a Gentile name anyway?

It is perhaps not so curious that shortly after the two had returned to Antioch there arrived some members from the Jerusalem church with the theological opinion that "unless you are circumcised according to the custom of Moses, you cannot be saved."

The arrival of these polemicists is too coincidental to go by unnoticed. Why such a timely appearance in Antioch? Had murmurs from the congregation in Antioch already reached Jerusalem? Had John Mark publicly expressed doubts about the new trends in Paul's thinking?

The debate about the Law and the Gospel increased. Was a Christian obliged to keep the Jewish dietary regulations? Were adult Gentile converts obliged to undergo the dangerous and demeaning rite of circumcision?

The controversy grew troublesome, then acrimonious, then unbearable. And it would go on—for years and years and years. On one occasion it would raise Paul to such a pitch of rage that he would express the hideous desire that the Judaizers pressing circumcision on Gentile converts would go on themselves and engage in self-castration. "I wish those who unsettle you would mutilate themselves!" (Galatians 5:12). Incidentally, the profound theological difficulty of evangelizing Gentiles outside the context of the Jewish Law while, at the same time, refusing to repudiate the Law—as the so-called antinomian movement would do later—is nowhere so clearly evidenced as in this torturous and ill-tempered epistle to the Galatians.

As the problem began to grow ungovernable in Antioch, the most logical recourse seemed to be an appeal to the "pillars" in Jerusalem for a judgment. So Barnabas, Paul and certain other delegates were sent down to the mother church for arbitration by the chief apostles. The issue, needless to say, was presented within the context of the over-all success of the Gentile mission.

And all the assembly kept silence; and they listened to Barnabas and Paul as they related what signs and wonders God had done through them among the Gentiles.

—Acts 15:12

The decision was rendered by James, the apostle who seems to have presided over the Jerusalem church. He wrote it out in a letter which was sent back to the church in Antioch by a return delegation from the Jerusalem church. This document is interesting not only for its support of Paul's position, but also because it is a quite masterful bit of compromise between two strongly held theological positions. Of greater import is the fact that for the church it proved to be a landmark decision.

. . . Since we have heard that some persons from us have troubled you with words, unsettling your minds, although we gave them no instructions, it has seemed good to us in assembly to choose men and send them to you with our beloved Barnabas and Paul, men who have risked their lives for the sake of our Lord Jesus Christ. We have therefore sent Judas and Silas, who themselves will tell you the same things by word of mouth. For it has seemed good to the Holy Spirit and us to lay upon you no greater burden than these necessary things; that you abstain from what has been sacrificed to idols and from blood and from what is strangled and from unchastity. If you keep yourselves from these, you will do well. Farewell.

—Acts 15:24–29

DIFFERING OPINIONS ON MARK

Long-ranging as the judgment of the Jerusalem church might have been, it had an immediate effect too. It whetted Paul's appetite for further missionary ventures. Now he could become a full-fledged apostle to the Gentiles. Now he could preach the Gospel without being hampered by the religious legalisms of his Judaism.

Paul had not been back in Antioch long when he suggested to Barnabas that they revisit the Christian colonies they had established on Cyprus as well as the mainland to the north. Barnabas agreed. But at the same time he proposed that once more they take his kinsman John Mark along.

Paul refused. John Mark had failed on a former occasion, he explained. He was not to be trusted.

Barnabas thought Paul's judgment too severe. Mark, after all, was scarcely more than a lad. He was entitled to make a few mistakes.

"No," one almost hears Paul saying. "Not when there is something so important as Christian truth at stake."

And there arose a sharp contention, so that they separated from each other; Barnabas took Mark with him and sailed away to Cyprus, but Paul chose Silas. . . .

—Acts 15:39–40

With these words Barnabas all but disappears from the pages of the New Testament. In his future epistles, Paul will refer to him on occasion. In I Corinthians he will allude to the fact that he and Barnabas always supported themselves on their missionary journey. Barnabas' name will appear three times in the letter to the Galatians in relation to the controversy over the Jewish question in Jerusalem discussed above. Paul will record that Barnabas acted "insincerely" in the matter, saying one thing and acting differently. What Paul probably meant is that Barnabas always maintained a strict adherence to the Law. Finally, in Colossians Paul will identify Mark as Barnabas' cousin.

But that is all. Paul, clearly, was not a sentimental person. There were more important things to write about than reminiscences of those incredible early days with Barnabas.

What happened to Barnabas after he sailed away to Cyprus with Mark is not known for sure. Clement places him in the Egyptian city of Alexandria for a time. Perhaps Barnabas died there. We cannot be sure. All we know is that in the act of taking the side of someone who had been misjudged, Barnabas moves beyond our view.

For Barnabas it seems an appropriate exit. And with it there disappears from the chronicles of the primitive church one of the finest and most genial apostles of them all.

Geniality aside, it must not be forgotten that in two extremely critical situations Barnabas turned out to be right. First he was right about one Saul of Tarsus, whom he supported against the fearful reservations of the Jerusalem apostles. Second, he was right about John Mark. Paul himself would come to realize this. In time there would be a reconciliation between Paul and Mark, and afterward Mark would become nearly indispensable to him.

The career of Barnabas reminds us once more that those "unremembered acts of kindness and of love" do have a way of shaping history. One wonders what might have happened if Barnabas had not given his generous and trusting support to the young Saul of Tarsus when he did. The thought staggers the mind! What would have happened to the church without a St. Paul? Or what kind of New Testament could have been put together without his letters?

Interestingly, there was another New Testament writer whose timely support by Barnabas was crucial. Suppose Barnabas had departed with Paul on that second missionary journey, leaving John Mark behind in disgrace? Could this young man have ever recovered from such callous treatment? Is it not likely that he would have fallen into any one of the hundred forms which despair can take? And recall that this was the person who would come to write the Gospel which bears his name—the very earliest of them all, and the one on which the other two synoptics heavily depend!

One is bound to see in Barnabas—this burly, lovable, Christlike man of compassion and forgiveness—a person without whom the New Testament may never have come to be.

Still one must admit that these possibilities are merely conjectures. And if that "good man" Barnabas had heard such speculations while he was yet alive, he may well have brushed them aside with a slow laugh and declared that what presently concerned him was that Demas be given another chance. Everyone, after all, stumbles once in a while.

L.I.F.E. College Library
1100 Glendale Blvd.
Los Angeles, Calif. 90026

XI LUKE THE UNKNOWN

Give honour unto Luke Evangelist;
For he it was (the aged legends say)
Who first taught Art to fold her hands and pray.
—Dante Gabriel Rossetti

A man dressed in a linen tunic and seated before a low table.

The room he occupies is a small one which leads off the atrium of the home of a minor Roman nobleman. The nobleman happens to be a secret Christian.

There is a latticed opening in the wall of the room through which is filtered the emerging light of day. It also admits the sounds of a Roman morning—the clatter of chariot wheels against the paving stones, the hooves of horses, the cries of farmers urging their donkeys toward the market places, the sounds of first greetings, the call of a child, the incessant clucking of hens.

The man listens to all of this with a subdued, almost painful joy. He is an elderly man with silver hair. Age has taught him to value the wonder of each new morning.

At length he turns his attention to the tabletop. Scattered over it are various scrolls. To one side are the various instruments of writing. Directly before him is a blank sheet of parchment.

*The man contemplates the work before him. His trea-
tise, he understands first of all, must begin with a dedication.
And not any ordinary dedication will do. This one must have
elegance. It must have style. It must be the sort of dedication
which will capture the admiration of a very influential senator
who has shown some interest in the new Christian faith,
and whose wife has already begun baptismal instruction.*

*Should this particular official be converted, the man at
the table tells himself, the Christian churches scattered about
the empire might receive some measure of official recognition. They will be designated as licit religious organizations.
It will mean the end of governmental harassment. The
chances of further incidents of sanctioned violence against
the brotherhood, such as that which occurred during the
reign of Nero Claudius Caesar when both Peter and Paul
lost their lives, would be greatly diminished.*

*The elderly man recalls his brief conversation with the
senator. There had been such an intense interest on the Roman's part in the founder of the religion. It was quite amazing,
considering that this founder had been one of those despised
Jews; and not only that, but had been put to death as a
criminal as well! Again and again he had asked questions
about the teachings, the healings, the reported wonders associated with this Jesus of Nazareth. Did he truly possess
such divine powers, the senator had asked, that he could
overcome the forces of death? And what was the proof of
it?*

*At one point in the conversation the Roman official had
directed his interest to the birth of Jesus. He said that
there was a long-standing tradition in Rome that the births
of men of destiny were invariably accompanied by various
portents. And what had been those which surrounded the
birth of this Palestinian worker of wonders?*

*The person seated at the table frowns a bit as he recalls
the incisive intelligence of the man. He was not the sort*

who accepted religion easily. His reason served as a power-
ful censor of every religious concept presented to him.

And yet, the elderly man mused, he had chosen as a
sort of literary nickname the Greek name of Theophilus.
It meant "one who loves God," which seemed to indicate
that for all his innate skepticism, the Roman senator was
truly a seeker of truth.

It was for such as Theophilus that the forthcoming work
was being written. It would be an account of Jesus' life
and the beginnings of the Church. Its chief appeal would
be to the "cultured despisers of religion" in Rome.

The man takes up his quill. He examines the condition
of its point before dipping it into the pot of ink. He
contemplates the very first sentence of all, then leans forward
and begins to write. . . .

A PENCHANT FOR OBSCURITY

Luke, the reputed author of the Gospel according to
St. Luke and the Acts of the Apostles, does not figure
large in the letters of Paul. Only twice is he mentioned for
certain. It was Paul's custom to end his letters with the
sundry greetings of his companions. It is among such that we
find Luke's name, though it is well down the list. In the
letter to the Colossians the name of Luke is preceded by
such virtual unknowns as Aristarchus, Jesus Justus and
Epaphras. We find a similar list of names at the conclusion
of Philemon. Here Luke's is last of all.

There is one more definite reference to him in the New
Testament which indicates a long-standing tradition in the
early Church that during a period of crisis in Paul's ministry,
when loyalties were torn this way and that, Luke remained
steadfast while Demas turned away.

It is the excessive modesty of the man which eventually

catches the attention, though it initially loses it, for those who do not push themselves to the fore are only regarded kindly, if at all. Until one's attention is drawn to the almost compulsive reticence of Luke, he is apt to be put in a niche labeled "beloved physician," after which all interest in him tends to cease.

No other personality of the Bible seems to have harbored such a conspicuous desire for anonymity. Luke had no hesitation in setting forth the work of Christ for all the world to see. His Gospel is an incredible panorama, joining heaven and earth in a manner which can hardly be regarded as less than breathtaking by believer and unbeliever alike. "The most beautiful book ever written," said Renan, though he didn't believe one-quarter of it.

In addition to the Gospel there is a sequel entitled "The Acts of the Apostles," although in fact it is only about Peter and Paul. Luke created a dyptich, setting alongside his Gospel narrative an account of the birth of the Church. Particular emphasis was given in the latter work to that aspect of the advent of Christianity which interested him most—the evangelization of the Gentiles.

His depiction of the blazing results of the day of Pentecost is huge and heroic—the sort of thing a Jacques Louis David would paint, filled with figures terrestrial and extra-terrestrial. The energetic figures in the foreground are Peter and Paul. About them are arranged a host of first generation Christians representing every shade of enthusiasm and virtue. But nowhere, not even in the darkest corner, do we find so much as a semblance of the work's progenitor. He does not even sign his name.

His extravagant modesty may account for the curious absence of the name of Titus from the Acts of the Apostles. Why this important Paulinist figure of the first years of witness among the Gentiles is not mentioned seems best accounted for by a suggestion made first by Origen in the third century,

then by Jerome in the fourth, to the effect that Titus and
Luke were brothers. It seems a likely explanation. Luke's
exceptional diffidence would have no doubt been applied
to the immediate members of his family as well.

It is through Paul that we discover that Luke was one of
his companions. Most likely it was Paul himself who converted him to the new Messianic religion which had arisen
so spontaneously in the environs of Jerusalem. Paul's glanc-
ing references to Luke indicate that the Apostle was rather
fond of, if not entirely impressed by, the man. "Greetings
to you from our dear friend Luke, the doctor," he writes
to the Colossians, fixing an unconscious esteem upon his
companion's easygoing disposition and medical abilities.

One is left with the impression that Luke must have
been one of those quiet, unassuming fellows whom the
intense, touchy shapers of history like Paul prefer having
around them. Besides, we have every indication that Paul
decidedly needed a physician in his retinue. He was afflicted
with a chronic illness of one sort or another, a "thorn in the
flesh" which would not leave him despite his most earnest
prayers for deliverance. The nature of that illness is not
known, though it seems most reasonable to assume that he was
the victim of one of the prevalent eye ailments of that part
of the world. Else why would he have dictated most of his
letters?

Whatever the nature of his malady, Paul must have leaned
heavily upon Luke for treatment. Luke's role in the missionary
journeys, therefore, may have been of critical importance.
It is by no means fantastic to presume that without the
medical services of Luke, Paul would have been restricted
in his travels. What the results of this eventuality might
have been are impossible to calculate.

Nevertheless, beyond his professional capacities, Luke
seems to have had little part in the actual work of evangelization. One puts two and two together and comes to the

conclusion that *this* evangelist, at any rate, must have been a rather tongue-tied fellow. There is no record of his having ever uttered so much as a word in public, though Paul no doubt had him try.

Paul may well have wondered why the Spirit didn't give the fellow a tongue. Luke, for his part, may have prayed desperately for the gift of easy, self-assured speech, but it never came. One is left with the probable assumption that he continued to blush furiously every time he was obliged to talk to more than two people at once, managed to accompany every word by at least two *ahs*, and altogether proved his unerring talent for making every sentence come out sounding like a cracked plate. In short, Luke was one of those whose every speech turned out to be a most forgettable experience.

Consequently, Luke learned to keep to the edges of the crowd. He had a way of blending, of not being noticed. Once in Philippi Paul and Silas were mobbed for driving a soothsaying spirit from some pathetic little slave girl. Luke was there all the time, but no one seemed to see him. As a result, Paul and Silas went to jail. But Luke did not.

There are plenty of indications that shyness was not the only handicap! Luke's most serious problem was that he was a Gentile; and while in theory there was supposed to be no difference between Jew and Gentile in the bond of Christ, the truth is that those early Gentile converts had great difficulty getting the hang of Jewish theology, especially the serpentine rabbinic theology of which Paul was master. Luke simply couldn't get the hang of it. No matter how often Paul drummed his complex doctrines into the young convert's ears, Luke always managed to miss the point, as the book of Acts demonstrates again and again. Luke would listen, all right. And he would probably smile and nod his head in assent as Paul patiently explained himself.

But all the while inside he must have been wondering what the fiery little man was talking about.

And Paul, who was one of history's most adept students of human nature, no doubt eventually came to realize that Luke simply could not understand, much less enjoy, the labyrinthine concepts of atonement and justification and imputed righteousness. Gentile minds just weren't arranged along these lines.

The result is that Paul probably gave up the effort and let Luke alone. The Spirit gave a variety of gifts, he came to conclude, and Luke's had to do with those of healing, and that was all.

Quite possibly the Apostle would catch sight of his physician friend scribbling away from time to time on scraps of parchment. Luke, he knew, was an inveterate diarist. But, the Apostle may have wondered to himself, what in the world could Luke find to write about?

As it turned out, Luke had a great deal to write about. And Paul would have been astonished had he lived to learn the outcome.

That travel diary of Luke pricks the interest. If he did keep one, and most scholars assume he did, what went into it? Just those matters which pertained to his itinerary?

It seems unlikely. Those who keep journals of their travels are a curious lot by nature, and given to writing down all sorts of irrelevant data. Is it not possible, then, that Luke jotted down many firsthand memories of Jesus' life that he heard here and there?

Such a question becomes very important when it is remembered that Luke's Gospel contains a great deal of unique material. The similarity of his Gospel to that of Mark and Matthew is well known. "Synoptic" is the term customarily used to describe the similarity of outlook and material in these three books. Yet it is widely recognized that Luke is fully as important for that which distinguishes it from the other synoptics as the resemblances, and leaves us with the obvious question, where *did* Luke get his special material (or *L*, as the scholars call it)? Could not this have been the result of years of note-taking in various parts of Asia Minor? It seems indeed a possibility, though by no means can it be proved.

A fragment of supporting evidence is to be found in Luke's passing reference to a visit of some duration with Philip and his "four unmarried daughters." Just why Luke included this episode in the Acts of the Apostles when so many other similar visits must have gone unmentioned is a mystery. Could it not be accounted for with the suggestion that it was Luke's way of indicating gratitude for the amount of data which came his way on this occasion? After all, four unmarried daughters must have a great deal to talk about!

One wonders if it were here that he heard the birth and infancy narratives which are peculiar to Luke? Or perhaps the parable of the Good Samaritan, which also appears only in the Third Gospel? Or a more complete account of Christ's post-resurrection appearances?

One possibility seems more certain than the others. Of all the Gospels, Luke's has the greatest wealth of information regarding the place of women in Christ's ministry and the early years of the Church. Surely Philip's spinster daughters might have had something to do with this!

When analyzing St. Luke, one is tempted to compare him with Boswell, leaving aside, of course, certain of the grosser proclivities of the eighteenth-century journalist. Both became fastened to great men. Both were scribblers. Both had a fine eye for detail. Both had many limitations despite their art, particularly cognitive ones, for both had difficulty understanding their mentors at their most profound.

Having to this point piled assumption on assumption, it seems only right to desist long enough to return to a prior

question. It is the most vital of them all; namely, was Luke
the Physician indeed the author of Luke and Acts?

This question could just as easily emanate from a Biblical
literalist as a "liberal." The former because nowhere in the
Scriptures proper is there the slightest indication that Luke
was the author of these works. The only thing we have to go
on is tradition, and the strict constructionist of the Bible
is notedly dubious about tradition!

As to the "liberal," he may well hail from those heydays
of Biblical criticism when any name on a Biblical document
was almost prima facie evidence that it was written by
someone else. Certainly for a time Luke became subject
to the doubts of Biblical scholars.

But alternatives nagged. If it wasn't Luke who wrote the
Third Gospel, then who? All sorts of informed guesses
were made about the origin of Luke-Acts, but the more the
argument raged, the more it looked like Luke was the author
after all. In the absence of any definite information one way
or another, the doubters were left with one devastating
question. Why, considering the early Church's compulsion to
have the name of a bona fide apostle at the head of every
book of the new Christian scriptures, had the Church Fathers been content to assign authorship to such an unap-
ostolic and obscure figure as Luke?

The all-but-certain conclusion, and the one assumed here,
is that from the beginning there has never been any doubt
that Luke, the companion of Paul, wrote the Gospel which
bears his name and the Acts of the Apostles.

They are important works, both in terms of content and
size. Together they comprise more than one-quarter of the
New Testament. The irony here is inescapable. To think
that the quiet and serene fellow with his bag of ointments
and salves should end by composing a larger portion of the
Christian scriptures than anyone else, Paul and John in-

cluded! The self-effacing Luke, in other words, turns out
to have been the major author of the New Testament!

It seems fitting to end our study of Biblical personalities
with this quiet and humble man, for in few others of the
known writers of the Bible does the idea of inspiration seem
so appropriate. Luke's patent efforts to suppress himself in
favor of his subject seems very near the heart of the doctrine
of Biblical inspiration.

In the pages to follow we shall examine more closely the
Evangelist's reticence, then proceed to some of the dis-
closures about himself which he let slip through. Finally
we shall attempt to reconstruct the manner by which Luke
composed his two treatises.

WHAT LUKE OMITTED

It is said that while most authors wish to reveal themselves by their writings, at least a few attempt to conceal
themselves by so doing.

Paul would certainly serve as an example of the former
tendency. Who, reading for example the second letter to the
Corinthians, could say otherwise? In every sentence the
religious convictions of one man, Paul, are evident.

Luke represents a contrast. As an author he is almost
conspicuous by his absence. In neither of the books assigned
to him is there the slightest reference to himself or his
personal concerns. The only indication that he bore any
relationship to the events he described is the occasional
use of the pronoun "we" in certain parts of the Acts of the
Apostles. In creating his dramatic account of the life of
Christ and the beginnings of the Church he included scores
and scores of characters. That Luke himself deserved some
small reference for his many years with Paul cannot be

gainsaid. Yet the fact is that Luke pointedly omitted the very mention of his name.

Beyond any conscious attempt at self-concealment, there even seems to lie other and deeper indications of the author's reticent nature. For example, it is possible that Luke attempted to conceal himself behind a confusing variety of literary styles. Biblical scholars have long noted the linguistic peculiarities of Luke-Acts. The writing could almost be the work of a half dozen people, for the style ranges from the polished Greek of the academy to the labored efforts of someone not quite at home with the lingua franca of the first century, koine Greek.

These variations in style pique the curiosity of those interested in the literary aspects of the New Testament. They wonder if they are dealing with a diffident mind, or an artistic and imitative one. The more that is known of Luke, the greater the likelihood that it is a combination of both.

One must allow that Luke was quite successful in his efforts to eliminate all traces of himself in his writing. Our biographical data concerning him is very scanty.

As a prime instance, we have no certain knowledge of where he came from—a factor of some significance when it is recalled that many in those days incorporated the place of their origin into their surnames. Was Luke from Syrian Antioch? This seems the most plausible answer. It was here, after all, that Barnabas with the help of Paul first established a flourishing church among the Gentiles. Here it was that adherents of "the way" were first called Christians. It was from the prosperous Antiochene Church that the first missionary journey was launched. And if Titus were indeed Luke's brother, then Antioch *must* have been Luke's hometown, for Titus was already a traveling companion of Paul by the time of the first missionary journey.

Yet one cannot rule out the evidence of those who argue

for Philippi. The basis for their belief is the supposition that the man from Macedonia who appeared to Paul by night asking for the Gospel to be preached in the regions around Philippi was none other than Luke himself. Lending credence to this theory is the fact that the famous "we passages" in Acts commence directly afterward.

It may have been on this occasion that Luke met Paul for the first time, surely a momentous event in the life of the author. It does not seem out of character for Luke to disguise the circumstances, suggesting that the whole thing had been a vision of Paul, not a flesh and blood encounter.

Whether Antioch or Philippi, Luke does not say. Nor does he give us the even more critical information of how he happened to become a Christian. Conversions in the first few decades of the Church's life tended to be spectacular affairs. Luke's could hardly have been otherwise, considering the consequences of a Gentile doctor's allying himself with what at that time was a small Jewish splinter movement.

How he must have wanted to tell that story! What effort it must have taken to refrain from writing of the most important happening in his life!

In addition to a silence about the circumstances of his conversion, we are left just as ignorant of another important moment in Luke's life; namely, his decision to give up his medical practice and become a traveling companion of Paul. We wonder what, besides Paul's medical needs, prompted him to do so. We wonder what he may have left behind in the way of family and friends. A later tradition has it that the man never married, though it must be remembered the religious idealization of the unmarried state settled in very early throughout the Church.

As to his position in Paul's entourage, we assume once more that his professional abilities and Paul's medical needs had at least some bearing on one another. What the extent

or nature of Paul's dependency upon Luke might have been,
however, we are not told, for in accordance with one of the
long-standing customs of the medical profession—an ethical
standard at least as old as Hippocrates (fifth century B.C.)
—Luke never revealed the nature of his patient's ills.

Luke's relationship to Paul seems to have deepened as
the years passed. The indications are that he was with Paul
during the Apostle's final years in Rome. Perhaps from time
to time he served as Paul's scribe.

We are not told if Luke witnessed Paul's martyr death,
though it seems likely that he did. His silence on the matter,
however, seems peculiar. We are forced to such questions
as: Was there to be a third treatise following Luke and
Acts, one which would tell of the death of Peter and
Paul? Or were their martyrdoms too harrowing to describe?
Or again, did Luke's conspicuous desire to assure the Roman
government that Christians were loyal and peaceful citizens
disallow the implicit criticism conveyed by an account of
Christians executed under that government?

Luke's career after Paul's death is as uncertain as the
rest, if not more so. At least some part of his life was
taken up with the composition of his Gospel and Acts.
But of the rest we cannot know.

There are any number of legends about his later life.
Like many shadowy figures of Christian antiquity, Luke
became the subject of much pious speculation. As might be
expected, later Christians felt sure that in time he must
have become a bishop. The trouble is that no consensus
was achieved as to where his episcopate was served. According to one tradition it was Alexandria. Another mentions
Laodicea. Whichever, one is still bound to wonder. Somehow Luke does not seem the bishop type.

As might be expected, the confusion which surrounds
him extends to the place and manner of his death. According to one tradition he died in Bithynia of natural causes

at the age of seventy-four. Another places his death in Ephesus. Still another claims that he died a martyr's death in Alexandria by beheading, while another maintains that it occurred at Rome during a mass slaughter.

One is almost forced to say that this type of reverent speculation only indicates the success with which Luke kept himself obscure. Indeed, so successful was Luke's veiling of himself that we cannot even say for sure *why* he entertained this passion for anonymity. Was it, as we have suggested all along, because he was possessed of an innately shy nature? Or could it be that he was motivated by a deep conviction that Jesus Christ alone should occupy the center of his efforts? Perhaps it was a bit of both. Or neither. No one can say.

Thus Luke remains an elusive quarry. Yet in some measure it is his very elusiveness which makes him so interesting. We can be grateful that he was not entirely successful in his efforts. As we shall now see, at least some of his very personal traits *do* come through his writings. Fortunately for us, they are traits which make the investigation worth while.

SOME UNCONSCIOUS SELF-REVELATIONS

As has been noted, we have, from a purely objective point of view, just four fragments of demonstrable historical information about Luke: first, that he was a companion of Paul; second, that he was regarded with considerable affection by those about him; third, that he was a physician; and fourth, that he was a Gentile.

By any biographical standards, the information is minuscule. Certainly it is much too meager to be the basis of any character study. And yet when we multiply these four fragments by the relatively certain fact that Luke was the author of the Third Gospel and the Acts of the Apostles, we suddenly find ourselves in the near vicinity of one of the most fascinating of all Biblical personalities.

The search for Luke's individuality is a circuitous one. One does not come upon him directly. He is nearly everywhere in the New Testament, and he is nowhere. The attempt to find him could be likened to the effort involved in one of those picture puzzles in which a face is concealed in the trees and clouds of a landscape. A few clues, an idea of what one should be looking for, some diligent inspection, and all at once the face emerges from its background.

In Luke's case we begin with the obvious—to wit, the firsthand information that he was a physician. What can be made of this fact?

In truth not a great deal. In the first century A.D. medicine was not the prestigious profession that it has since become. As is well known, up until the eighteenth century the practice of medicine was a highly inexact science. Indeed, in retrospect it could hardly be regarded as a science at all. It was rather a mixture of presumptions and skills which, at best, was directed toward the treatment of surface wounds and sores, the setting of broken bones and various simple forms of surgery. It is such skill that the fifth-century B.C. Athenian vase-painter Sosias illustrates in his depiction of a warrior having his wounds bandaged in what seems to be a very skillful and up-to-date manner.

The cause and cure of internal disease, on the other hand, remained clouded by ignorance. On the whole, organic disorders were thought to be caused by evil spirits, or an imbalance of the physical components which made up the body—the so-called "tempers." Such ailments were then treated by a variety of nostrums or incantations, with the result that people were generally cured despite, rather than because of, their treatment.

In view of the general lack of medical information, we are left with the dolorous likelihood that the medical profession in those days swarmed with quacks and the credulous. It is for this reason that Paul's adjective "beloved" (ὁ ἀγαπητὸς, literally the one worthy of love) takes on added importance.

Without meaning to shake the life out of the term, or to read more into it than the Apostle intended, it nevertheless seems worth suggesting at this point that the word "beloved" could very neatly describe one of the general categories in which physicians even today are placed by the laity. This category is easily recognized when it is set in perspective with others.

For example, an alternative category into which other physicians are often placed is that for which the term "skillful," or "competent," is often employed. Such physicians are sometimes regarded as cold and intellectual. Their approach to medical practice is that of the expert, the aloof clinician, the one whose attention is fastened onto the problem rather than the patient. A physician of this nature is often abrupt with those who are ill. As a consequence, he may be respected by all, but is rarely beloved by anyone.

Another generally recognized category of physicians is that of charlatan. He is the worst of all, neither beloved nor skillful. This is the type of doctor who takes up the profession so that he can make a great deal of money. He is a parasite, who enriches himself at the expense of human suffering, or through exploiting the fears of those who are neurotically preoccupied with their health. His vocation is one long perjury. He is dishonest both by the diagnoses he gives and the placebos he dispenses. Today most medical charlatans are simply fakes. Still there are some, such as the various "Dr. Feelgoods" with their hypodermics filled with amphetamines, who have genuine medical degrees and are licensed to practice.

Against these two categories stands that which is quite appropriately defined by the term "beloved." In current attitudes, a physician of this sort is likely to be referred to in such terms as "the old family doctor." What one means by the phrase is the doctor who is just as concerned with the patient as the illness, who refuses to divorce the two, and whose deep compassion for sufferers makes him tireless in his efforts to bring about cures.

It is in this latter category that Luke seems to belong. Such is the tribute paid him by the Apostle Paul, and Paul's estimate is reinforced by the manifest sympathy displayed by Luke in his writings for those struck down by injury or disease. One of his most characteristic stories is that which tells of how some friends of a sick man literally tore the roof off a house so that they could lower their friend into Jesus' healing presence. Such feelings of desperation must have haunted Luke in his futile treatment of the incurably ill.

Luke did not fail to appreciate the priority which Jesus gave to the relief of physical suffering, or the fact that this was given a higher priority than religious obligation.

One Sabbath he was teaching in a synagogue, and there was a woman there possessed by a spirit that had crippled her for eighteen years. She was bent double and quite unable to stand up straight. When Jesus saw her he called her and said, "You are rid of your trouble." Then he laid his hands on her, and at once she straightened up and began to praise God. But the president of the synagogue, indignant with Jesus for healing on the Sabbath, intervened and said to the congregation, "There are six working-days: come and be cured on one of them, and not on the Sabbath." The Lord gave him his answer: "What hypocrites you are!" he said. "Is there a single one of you who does not loose his ox or his donkey from the manger and take it out to water on the Sabbath? And here is this woman, a daughter of Abraham, who has been kept

prisoner by Satan for eighteen long years: was it wrong for her
to be freed from her bonds on the Sabbath?"

—St. Luke 13:10–16

For many years it was believed that the writings of
Luke were filled with medical terminology. Later study
modified this belief, though it may be wondered in the
first place why Luke should be expected to strew his
writings with technical terms any more than would be expected of such more recent physician-writers as Somerset
Maugham and Lloyd Douglas. Nevertheless, what can hardly
be avoided when reading Luke's Gospel is the profound
interest of the author in the healing aspects of Christianity.
How greatly the "beloved physician" must have been attracted to the "great physician" can be inferred from Luke's
awed description of Christ: "and the power of the Lord
was with him to heal the sick" (Luke 5:17).

It is not at all surprising that Luke's compassion for the
sick should similarly extend to the wicked. It could be said
that he regarded sin as more of the nature of illness rather
than any deliberate disobedience. For Luke it was almost
a case of a person's catching sin and dying, for which he
deserved not condemnation but pity. Adolf Harnack's remark
about Luke is illuminating: "He has a boundless—indeed a
paradoxical—love for sinners, together with the most confident
hope of their forgiveness and amendment."

Before proceeding to two somewhat overlooked traits in
Luke's personality, we might here make the general comment
that for all his shyness, Luke seems to have been an educated,
urbane individual. Clergy often make much of the presump-
tion that Christianity at first was the religion of simpletons,
for which the term "simple people" is more customarily
used. This may be doubted. There is little reason to assume
that the disciples were unintelligent, though they may have
lacked formal education. And if the Church began as "the

religion of slaves," at least not all of these slaves were un-
lettered and ignorant, as Luke's writing amply demonstrates.

One rather interesting sidelight on Luke's personality is
his evident sense of humor. This trait may have been one of
the reasons Paul cherished him so, for humorless Paul must
have been transfixed by anyone who could laugh in the
midst of a troubled and fallen world.

Luke's selection of parables shows his appreciation for
the keen wit and insight of Jesus. The story of the cunning
steward who was a rascal to the very end must have
brought several chuckles to one who was as inclined to
laugh at human foibles as Luke obviously was. And the
story of the unjust judge who feared neither God nor man,
but in time came to cringe at the sight of a shrewish woman
possessed of an incredible talent for relentless nagging,
is one which only a good-humored biographer would be apt
to include in such a generally serious biography.

Finally, no one but a person with a merry heart could
relate the story of how the Jews in Rome told Paul on his
arrival that the only thing they knew about Christianity was
"that no one has a good word to say for it" (Acts 28:22).

A second trait worth noting is Luke's obvious fascination
with ships and the sea. It is because of this that we are,
for example, given the delightful, but otherwise unimpor-
tant, information that on one occasion Paul traveled on a
ship named *Castor and Pollux*, whose home registry was
Alexandria.

The "we passages" of Acts never fail to provide vivid
descriptions of the manner in which a journey was made.
For Luke it was never a matter of *going* to Samothrace. One
may have made a "straight run to Samothrace," but one
never simply *went* there.

Luke's love and awe of the sea is nowhere more evident
than in his description of Paul's final journey to Rome. The
following passages demonstrate this most clearly. Note the

evangelist's knowledge of nautical matters, the precision with which he indicates the points of navigation, as well as his evident fascination with the power of the sea and the wind.

Leaving Sidon we sailed under the lee of Cyprus because of the headwinds, then across the open sea off the coast of Cilicia and Pamphylia, and so reached Myra in Lycia. . . . Then, as the wind continued against us, off Salmone we began to sail under the lee of Crete, and, hugging the coast, struggled on to a place called Fair Havens, not far from the town of Lasea. . . . But before very long a fierce wind, the "North-easter" as they call it, tore down from the landward side. It caught the ship and, as it was impossible to keep head to wind, we had to give way and run before it. We ran under the lee of a small island called Cauda, and with a struggle managed to get the ship's boat under control. When they had hoisted it aboard, they made use of tackle and undergirded the ship. Then, because they were afraid of running on to the shallows of Syrtis, they lowered the mainsail and let her drive. Next day, as we were making very heavy weather, they began to lighten the ship; and on the third day they jettisoned the ship's gear with their own hands. For days on end there was no sign of either sun or stars, a great storm was raging, and our last hopes of coming through alive began to fade.

—Acts 27:4–5, 7–8, 14–20

Luke's conclusion of his account of the shipwreck could have almost been written by a nineteenth-century Nantucket whaler.

When day broke they could not recognize the land, but they noticed a bay with a sandy beach, on which they planned, if possible, to run the ship ashore. So they slipped the anchors and let them go; at the same time they loosened the lashings of the steering-paddles, set the foresail to the wind, and let her drive to the beach. But they found themselves caught between cross-currents and ran the ship aground, so that the

bow stuck fast and remained immovable, while the stern was
being pounded to pieces by the breakers.

—Acts 27:39–42

THE WRITING OF LUKE AND ACTS

At this point we turn a closer scrutiny on Luke's career
as an author, and one of the first and most important factors
to bear in mind is that it was not his intention to write for
posterity. Luke would have been quite amazed had he been
told the outcome of his work—that it would be read by
countless generations yet to be born, translated into every
conceivable sort of language, pored over by vast armies of
scholars, memorized by the devout, and in time achieve the
status of being one of the major written influences over
the mind of man. Had Luke, given his personality, any
notion that this might come to pass, he might have found
it impossible to pick up his pen, his hand would have
trembled so.

The circumstances under which these two treatises came
to be written were quite different. Luke's aims were very
modest indeed. It was his intention to write *to* a rather select
group of people, and *for* a particular reason. As he wrote,
he kept the general outlook of his readership in mind. He
was quite aware of their prejudices, their inclinations, their
limitations, their likes and dislikes. As any good writer should,
he made every effort to be persuasive. He anticipated his
readers' objections, he appealed to their sensibilities, he made
every effort to fathom their deepest interests and to address
himself to those interests.

The point must be emphasized, for it stands in sharp
contrast to the widely held and erroneous belief that the
New Testament writers were somehow aware of the universal
import of their work. Such attitudes are reflected in those

much-admired paintings which are supposed to depict the Biblical authors at work. The settings in these paintings could be described as ivory tower Gothic. The writer sits in splendid isolation. He is totally removed from all ordinary human congress. He is rendered as a pallid-faced scholar, and is posed in a languid posture with a pen about to fall from his fingers.

What the painter is trying to convey is the impression that the author is in the process of being inspired, that he is about to engrave divine truths for endless generations yet unborn. The eyes are upcast and staring. Visions hover about the head. One senses that the majestic Elizabethan words are slowly beginning to take form in his brain, and that shortly he will collapse forward onto the desk and dash off the eighth verse of the fourth chapter.

Such idealized depictions of the composition of Holy Writ bear little relationship to what must have been the fact. With a few notable exceptions, most Biblical writers seem to have been busy men of affairs who, when they wrote, generally had some definite reason for doing so.

This is particularly true of the New Testament, and in some measure distinguishes it from the Old, which tends to possess a much more self-conscious recognition of its canonical possibilities.

As for Luke, there can be no genuine appreciation, much less comprehension, of his writings without the recognition that they began as mundane, practical expositions of Christian backgrounds. The quickest way to gain an appreciation of Luke's work is to imagine oneself the mysterious Theophilus of the first verse, for it was to this person—in all probability a Roman official of breeding and education—that Luke addressed himself, and not to twentieth-century Christians.

Before dealing specifically with what might have been Luke's objectives in writing his two works, we are almost obliged to take on a prior and, in some respects, more intriguing question. To wit, why were *any* of the Gospels written? What were the conditions which called them forth? What developments in the early Church brought about the need for these four accounts of the life and ministry of Jesus? What compelled an obscure companion of Paul to write as he did?

These questions are intriguing ones because we can be fairly certain that the first generation of Christians felt no particular need for a comprehensive written narrative of the life of Christ. The reason seems obvious. It is that for the first few decades of the Church's life, the story of Jesus remained largely in the possession of those who could speak from firsthand experience. A great many of those first Christians had actually seen Jesus. They had heard his words of healing and acceptance. They had followed him. They had mourned his death. They had undergone the incredible experiences of Easter and Pentecost.

For at least twenty years after its birth, the Church was endowed with a considerable number of people who could provide living corroboration of the truth of the Gospel. This fact is illustrated in one of Paul's letters to the Corinthians where he declares that most of some five hundred men who had seen the risen Lord were yet alive.

There is yet another and even more profound reason why the earliest Christians felt no need for a documentary about Christ. It was their belief in his imminent return. Not one of that first generation of Christians could have possibly conceived of the Church's continuing for some two thousand years. They were convinced that they lived at the end of an age. They felt that the world was about to come to an end, that Jesus would shortly appear in the clouds of heaven and inaugurate the millennium.

It would be difficult to overstate the apocalyptic fervor which gripped the Church in those first years. So certain were those believers that the Second Coming was about to occur that at one point Paul was obliged to scold certain persons in the Church at Thessalonica who had given up working and begun to loaf as they awaited Judgment Day. Their argument must have been, Why wait? Why keep busy at things when the Kingdom of God is apt to break in on us at any moment?

One of the results of all this anticipation must have been a lack of interest in providing religious information for posterity. They simply felt no need for an official, that is, apostolic account of Jesus' life, passion and resurrection.

This does not mean that there were no Christian documents whatever in use among the various churches. Besides the Scriptures of the Old Testament, there were undoubtedly a sprinkling of writings which had to do with specifically Christian matters: songs, poems, stories, prayers, creeds, letters such as those of Paul and so forth.

Luke himself seems to have had access to a collection of Jesus' sayings which apparently achieved a rather wide circulation. This catalogue was likely the result of some perceptive person's recognition that a man's exact words were a highly perishable commodity, and so fixed those of Jesus into writing. Scholars have only been able to deduce the existence of this document from external evidence. There are, of course, no extant copies. This hypothetical document goes by the name of *Q*, from the German *Quelle* ('source').

Fragmentary and localized as these Christian writings were, they sufficed for a strange breed of people who never went to bed at night without wondering if the world would be around when they awakened.

It was the *delay* of the Second Advent, and the problems which that delay provoked, which became the precipitating factor in the writing of the Gospels. By the latter third of the first century there began to appear gaps in the number of those who remembered Calvary, and the empty tomb, and Pentecost, and all the rest. The old authority for the

L.I.F.E. College Library
1100 Glendale Blvd.
Los Angeles, Calif. 90026

truth of what was being said about those eventful days was slowly being eroded by the death of the old guard. There came a time when very few could speak of these matters from firsthand knowledge.

The result was that the stories about Jesus began to be embellished, which is another way of saying that they began to decay. What is worse, they suffered the misfortune of falling into the hands of enthusiasts and ax-grinders.

The problem reached a critical stage with the deaths of Peter and Paul during the reign of the jaded tyrant Nero. These two had achieved a certain preeminence in the Church. One served as an authority in matters of recollection. The other, a Pharisee by background, took care of doctrine. According to their various gifts, each served as a living corroboration of the truth about Christ. Peter and Paul served as standards against which the inevitable speculations and distortions in the new religion were measured. The effect of their deaths upon the Church must have been immense.

One supposes that initially there came a surge of apocalyptic expectation. Surely Christ would not delay his return with both Peter and Paul gone!

But as the years continued their ordinary way, and the heavens remained enigmatically closed, there began to come the sober realization that the Kingdom might not come so soon as hitherto believed. Meanwhile, there was a new generation of Christians growing up without any apostolic criteria by which their religious beliefs could be gauged. Clearly needed was some standardized account of the Church's recollection of Christ's life and ministry and death and resurrection. It would have to be both written and accepted as the sort of documentation to which Peter and Paul and the other apostles would give their unreserved approval.

Mark lost no time in taking up the task. He had been an associate of both Peter and Paul, so his credentials were faultless. Within a few years of the two martyrdoms, Mark had produced his Gospel. A part of his purpose seems to have been the attempt to provide comfort and resolution for early Christians as they began a painful recovery from the wounds inflicted by Nero. But more than this, Mark clearly intended to create an apostolic—for which read "authoritative"—account of Christian beginnings.

Mark's was the first Gospel, the one against which all others would eventually be measured. If it had been a comprehensive work, it may well have been the only Gospel to be included in the New Testament canon. Mark, however, apparently suffered certain defects in the eyes of the earliest fathers of the Church. In the first place, it seems to have been hurriedly done. Certain blocks of important information were missing. Moreover, the style was somewhat crude. Mark had a way of blurting things out. He also had the irritating tendency to repeat himself. Occasionally his grammar faltered.

Mark's Gospel could be likened to a rough draft. It contained the germinal idea. But it was incomplete. To those acquainted with the apostolic tradition, Mark needed finishing—more information, better organization, a certain amount of literary polish.

Luke's effort followed Mark's by some ten or fifteen years. While it cannot be known for certain what prompted Luke to his work, there is at least some evidence for the possibility that Luke was concerned to present apostolic Christianity to various persons in Roman officialdom who had shown some measure of interest in the Church. There are even indications that certain members of the emperor's court had become secret adherents of the faith. Tombstone inscriptions from this period show that at least a few highly placed Romans had become believers. It was to and for this group that Luke may have written his treatises. Indeed, it is quite possible that he wrote at the behest of one of them.

It is well to remember in connection with the writing of Luke-Acts that the conversion of Roman nobility to the Christian faith was not only a desirable goal from a missionary point of view. It was also a matter of some practical urgency. Already in the first century, while still an infant organization, the Church had been roughed up by suspicious Roman authorities. The general feeling in the capital was that Christians were a seditious lot, a belief which tended to be heightened by the resolute refusal of Christians to regard the genius of the emperor as being in any sense divine. Persecution resulted.

It may be because of this that we encounter in Luke's writings the muted themes of brotherhood and civic loyalty. Luke tried very hard to convince Roman officials that Christians were patriotic, though not religiously so—a point of distinction which has proved troublesome ever since.

In writing his Gospel and the Acts of the Apostles, Luke had a variety of resource materials. By comparing the various Gospels, Biblical scholars have been able to reconstruct with all but certain accuracy the manner in which Luke pieced these materials together. The following formula has been used to describe the process.

$$(Q+L)+\text{Mark}+\text{Birth Stories}+\text{Preface}=\text{Luke}$$

Taking this equation in order, Q, as previously noted, represents the sayings source. L is the material which is peculiar to Luke. Q and L were then combined with Mark's Gospel. It should be noted here that Luke's utilization of this Gospel only accounts for approximately one-third of his own, so it can hardly be said that Luke is merely a reworking of Mark. Furthermore, when Mark was used, Luke went to evident pains to edit and refine the earlier Gospel.

A further step in assembling his Gospel was the addition of a tradition regarding Christ's birth, which is only to be found in Luke. Finally there came his own brief dedication to the aforementioned Theophilus.

The second of the treatises is a more personal work. Much of Luke's information contained in the Acts of the Apostles was of a firsthand nature. The remaining materials may well have been jotted down from time to time in his journal. These included various reminiscences, sermons, fragments of liturgy and the like.

It is generally believed that Luke did his writing some time during the eighth decade of the first century. There is no absolute certainty about the locale, though one can hardly avoid the likelihood of Rome.

One of the more widespread impressions among Church people is that Luke and Acts were written by a young man. This may be because Luke was still fairly young when he accompanied Paul on his journeys. And yet if Luke were an established physician at the time of his conversion, presumably during the forties, he must have been a venerable senior of the Church when he sat down to write his account of the incredible events which took place from the birth of Christ until Paul's journey to Rome.

Of exceeding modesty, possessed of a gentle sense of humor, hopeful, persevering, faithful, Luke the Evangelist wrote so that his persecutors would believe. Of the author himself we know little. But because of him we know a great deal about Christ. And what more could any Christian ask?

. . . The author to Theophilus: Many writers have undertaken to draw up an account of the events that have happened among us, following the traditions handed down to us by the original eyewitnesses and servants of the Gospel. And so I in my turn, your Excellency, as one who has gone over the whole course of these events in detail, have decided to write a connected narrative for you, so as to give you authentic knowledge about the matters of which you have been informed.

In the days of Herod king of Judaea. . . .

L.I.F.E. College Library
1100 Glendale Blvd.
Los Angeles, Calif. 90026